SIN and the New American Conscience

SIN

and the New American Conscience

WILLIAM A. EMERSON, Jr.

Harper & Row, Publishers

New York, Evanston, San Francisco, London

SIN AND THE NEW AMERICAN CONSCIENCE.
Copyright © 1974
by William A. Emerson, Jr.
All rights reserved. Printed in the United States of America. No part of this book may be used or reproduced in any manner whatsoever without written permission except in the case of brief quotations embodied in critical articles and reviews. For information address Harper & Row, Publishers, Inc., 10 East 53rd Street, New York, N.Y. 10022. Published simultaneously in Canada by Fitzhenry & Whiteside Limited, Toronto.

FIRST EDITION

Designed by C. Linda Dingler

Library of Congress Cataloging in Publication Data

Emerson, William A   1923–
   Sin and the new American conscience.

   Includes bibliographical references.
   1. United States—Moral conditions. I. Title.
HN90.M6E46 1974   301.41′7973   74–4631
ISBN 0–06–062241–5

FOR
My children, Laura, Lucy, Ellen, Bill,
John and my son-in-law, Syd Alexander

I am grateful to my wife, Lucy, who has been
my faithful and tireless companion in this
curious trip through life and recollection. I
would not have enjoyed this passage alone.

CONTENTS

PROLOGUE

Middle age is a lookout. Unexpectedly, the foliage breaks and the ground drops away. You suck in your breath, and right before you is the landscape of your life. The scenery that you have been a part of is laid out, plunging, curving, and rolling away from you. There it all is. It is fantastic to see it this way, to comprehend almost visually your beginning and your end. From this height it is nearly possible to see around the last curve of one's own piece of existence. Up the last rise the silent cadence of time became audible, a melancholy sort of drumbeat. Most of us who are about fifty hang on to this ledge, slightly winded, drinking in the new perspectives.

It is a helluva view, and a great part of it is behind the eyes. What a trip it has been! And as I reflect on it, like all other travelers, I have a restlessness to go back to the familiar places. I want to hear the voices again and see the faces. I could flag down a Trailways bus and follow this yearning. But all I'd find is that I have changed. What I have left behind and miss is that part of life itself that is past and gone. At this point what I do have is a new consciousness and the experience of a very unlikely trip.

After all, I have carried certain things along with me. I could no more get rid of what has happened to me than I could get rid of my own skin. I was born in the simple, old RFD America —it is as incomprehensible looking back as these days would have been in prophecy. Those days back then were handmade. All adults felt responsible for all children, and a man's word was his bond. Distances were great and trips were celebrated. Automobiles had little vases of fresh flowers in them. Ice water was a significant drink, and there was absolutely no money.

We lived in a three-storied universe. God, with a long white beard, was on the top floor; we were in the middle; and Satan, with hooves and a forked tail, was on the bottom floor, flicking up splinters and poking the rafters. I frequently thought that I might die and go to hell. What would an awkward child do there? How long was eternity?

Life was heavy with a sense of sin. First of all, sin was breaking any of the Ten Commandments, whatever they meant. And it was doing anything that your parents called a sin. From church I picked up the fact that there was one sin for which you could not be forgiven. My mother encouraged me by saying that if you thought you were guilty of that sin, you probably weren't. Exemplars of rectitude were highly available to a small boy in a Calvinist world, and all of this provided a great contrast for sexual fantasies. Afterwards there could be remorse and guilt.

All in all, the mood of the members of the family was cheerful, excepting the archetypical ancient cousin who was a retired missionary. She wore a faded purple dress, and she knelt and prayed with you wherever you both were. When anybody got a new dress or suit or anything, she always wept. Material things were a snare. Little did she know. She had a musty smell like a small-town museum.

Sundays were so dense and boring, you couldn't cut them with a bread knife. You couldn't play baseball on Sunday; the town police would stop you. Down in the South in those days there were no movies on Sunday, and you couldn't have gone if there had been. Big-Little books could be read only on week-days, and the dirty little comic books were as dangerous to carry around as heroin is today. Daydreaming was about the liveliest entertainment that you could hope to get away with on Sunday, but you felt that you ought to keep them clean.

I remember distinctly that the penny had worth and dignity in those days. And, thinking of fiscal matters, I also remember that directly on the route to buy penny candy was a house that was owned and occupied by a lady who was a millionaire. The fact of this was electrifying to me. It was a gray-shingled, box-shaped house on a green, quiet street in Charlotte, North Carolina, and although I haven't seen the house in forty years, I could find it today with no trouble. What I have never since been able to find is that peculiar, spiritual overcast that colored our minds during the Great Depression. The grip of the depression is captured for me by the shock of one bit of information: the family who lived next door had such a hard time that *they had to eat their pet rabbit.* My mother said she was sorry I had been told about it.

I grew up skinny, picking my way through tough, unfamiliar schools, situated in neighborhoods that were full of low-grade violence. A great sport was to gang up on a boy and take his pants off; packs of boys roamed the playgrounds looking for victims during recess. One of the rougher gangs stripped boys and girls and dumped them together. This was ahead of its time, and it was pure murder. I do remember one junior-high princi-pal who carried a regulation blackjack in his hip pocket. I be-lieve it was for self-defense.

Back then, just for the sheer love of it, the police would go down into "nigger town" on their days off and beat the blacks. They would work with a club in one hand and a gun in the other. In many little and not-so-little Southern towns, no black man guilty of anything worse than running a stop sign ever arrived at the police station conscious. Those were mean days for folks who were the wrong color or unlucky. When high-school girls got knocked up, they either married the boy or the family moved out of town. If you couldn't go back to the farm, it wasn't that easy to get situated in another town.

I remember the lonely summer nights in Atlanta at grand-mother's house; lying in bed with the familiar reflections on the wall, I'd strain to hear the family noises downstairs. Then suddenly the umpah of the German-American Bund marching band would fill the night with brass that was as bright as sparks. I didn't know it, but they were warming up the audience for World War II. When I think of the music coming through the thickets of the center of that block, I can still see the hiding places where the bootleggers used to stash their white light-ning. If the grown folks asked the bootleggers how old their stuff was, they would wrinkle their eyes and laugh and say, "Have you got your watch on?" When they caught them—which was seldom because they were great wheel men—they went away to the federal pen. That's always the nicest jail in town.

Those were the days. Prosperity finally came creeping back from Appomattox and then was chased off the place by the boll weevil and the depression. Work was scarce, but it was sacred; and up north, vice-presidents of banks were jumping out of skyscrapers. The Protestant Work Ethic was the house religion of the Industrial Revolution. All men were chauvinist pigs. Only the advent of radio could reduce the incidence of insanity among farm wives. And, as they said, radio then was no more than a cat's whisker and a crystal.

Trees on which people had been lynched were landmarks of uncommon interest here and there. I can recall seeing the cuffs of policemen's pants below the sheets of Klansmen. And we had some fiery cross burnings on top of Stone Mountain, that great outcropping of granite on the outskirts of Atlanta. Once a drunk tumbled down the sheer face of that mountain and landed on the end of General Robert E. Lee's nose. He didn't even break the whiskey bottle in his back pocket.

Times were hard, things were simple; but people took care of each other, and nobody locked their doors. I've lived in places where you could put a brick over the edge of a five-dollar bill and leave it outside for a week. It was safer than the banks in those days. And I remember when the bulldog bit the Buttermilk Lady back in Raleigh, North Carolina, in 1930, but I have just recently forgotten her name. His name was Buster. She was the last great entrepreneur who sold buttermilk from door to door. Accountability and marketing have changed over the years, but dog bites are pretty much the same.

I speak as a white, middle-class, Southern-born male. I grew up in a comprehensible time and place. I heard the street cry of the cantaloupe man as a boy and lived to hear the blast-off of Apollo 11. The old America is imprinted on me, but I saw that rocket leave the earth and radicalize everybody's mind who was aware of the event. That lightning-sucking tornado of air and light separated that last old era from this new one. In less than a lifetime, America has changed from a rural to an urban nation. We have picked our people up out of one frame of mind and set them down in another one. Somewhere between the Buttermilk Lady and the moon landings we turned a corner and began a process of fateful change.

Our sense of sin is lost and found. It disappears but turns up again disguised as guilt. A new American conscience is evolving in a most painful way. The fact that we are getting it proves that we have been able to make crisis and agony useful to us as a nation. For the past thirty-five years our conscience has been like a damaged liver—it faithfully maintains a record of the past but meets the experience of the day uncertainly. We have just begun to see the confusion lift about right and wrong.

It is hard to get a clear view of the moral landscape from where we stand, but there is every indication that we are at a divide. We have had second thoughts, and we have reconsidered. I believe that there has been more popular concern about moral behavior in the last few years than in the whole rest of the century. This is part of the process of being reborn.

My profession has kept me involved in national affairs, and I have been under the rainspout of controversy about the tormentous questions of our time. These years have within them real possibilities of mass conversion to higher moral values. As I try to understand what has happened to me, I see that what has perplexed and harried us the most is full of good portent. There will be a requirement in the new American conscience that we become a more moral people. I can see this happening.

1

VIOLENCE
Order and Disorder

I suppose that everybody remembers where they were when they got the news. Three of us were having lunch in midtown Manhattan at Le Marmiton in its old location, when the first, stunned, broken announcements were made over radio. President Kennedy had been shot in Dallas. First there were inconclusive, deadly fragments that left you with a little, barely breathing hope. Being a newsman I knew that when the worst possible thing happens this is what you hear first. I wouldn't accept the message.

My associate, Otto Friedrich, and I got up from the table, and left our guest, a New York literary agent, behind. And we walked back to the office of the *Saturday Evening Post;* we both felt disembodied. But, as we walked, we began planning how we would tear up the magazine that was going to press at that moment, and try to report what had happened. We had to accept the reality ourselves before we could reach outside for anything else.

The president was dead. We went on from there to immerse ourselves in every breaking detail, in the scene and action of the shooting, in the crumbling disbelief of the people, in the cries of anguish and of inhumanity. There were even gleeful comments—back in Texas, somewhere, a teacher told her class, and they clapped. Symbolically, we were gathering all of the necessary fragments of the era that had just been smashed so we could bury them. An old reality was gone, and a new reality was coming together fast. We had to record it; so we never got out of the terrible news for three days and three nights. I began internalizing the death of John Kennedy then, and looking back I am amazed to find myself calling it *the first of the assassinations.*

Then it was unthinkable that an American president in our time would be assassinated, not *could be,* but *would be.* Now it is not unthinkable at all. And his successors in office have been called bold or foolhardy when they plunged into boisterous crowds to do a little hand-to-hand politicking. Since then, in recurrent nightmarish attacks, three of our most charismatic leaders have been killed or seriously wounded. Martin Luther King, Jr., Robert Kennedy, and George Wallace are a striking triumvirate. They are gut-rooted Americans, curiously archetypical of three of the major forces in the eternal American scramble for social and political balance. Targets of love and hate, Martin, Bobby, and George were the lightning rods of these stormy times. They drew the violence right out of the flammable air. It is almost as if they literally attracted sparks that set off the explosions that blew them up and damaged our society.

The death of John Kennedy left me feeling soiled, as if I, personally, had been partly responsible. I think this may be because I am a violent man; the fury is inside of me, and in recognizing my own violence, by extension I felt a part of all of the violence in our national lives.

Acts and events may be devastating, but they aren't immaculate conceptions. They come out of our violent insides. Violent actions and violent feelings are not the same. Nevertheless, we up the bidding until the atmosphere is so charged that it happens. We are always being conned into buying violence that we find we don't want. That we don't agree with. This happened fantastically in the South during the civil rights struggles of the '50s. It happened at Kent State. It happened at Watergate, which was pure violence. It is our big export, and it kept on happening in Vietnam. As embodied in events, continuous and instantaneous, it is surprising how violence has characterized the fateful events in our nation in the last thirty-five years.

We beat our blacks and blow up their children; we shoot our students; we rip off the constitutional rights of our individual citizens; we suppress our women and bully our children. We turn our whole firepower loose on a rural, backward nation in an unconstitutional war, but then something very significant happens.

We do it and then we see it. We look in the face of the mourning girl at Kent State. We see the little naked girl burning with napalm running down the road in Vietnam. The narcs break into the homes of innocent people, brutalize them, and destroy their property; we witness it. We see the dead fish in the polluted river and the earth stripped back from the green mountainside. We see what our inside violence does when we let it out, and we can't live with what we see.

Our perception is changed. We have second thoughts. Our consciousness is raised. We have some sort of deathbed conversion: **if this is what it takes, forget it!**

Being in the process of rebirth, we see our old selves for the first time. We are bloody-minded and we know it. We may be ill at ease with this description, but the rest of the world can easily agree that we are a violent people. This sort of awareness is slow breaking. It is extraordinary how long it takes for action to settle out of the solution of events and collect on the conscience of the individual. We dropped atomic bombs on Hiroshima and Nagasaki about thirty years ago, and the awesome implications of this have been working through the American conscience ever since.

We got the first real fallout only a few years ago, and since then there has been a slow-blossoming awakening of the mass of our people. Whether or not thermonuclear weapons were justified is not the question. Theoretically, millions of Japanese and American lives would have been lost in a conventional assault on the Japanese mainland. The question is, How can you live with an act that kills fifty, sixty, seventy thousand people and mutilates numberless more, born and unborn? What does this do to you? What does it do to the condition of man?

The full horror struck a few minds at the time. They were uncommon people or prophets, that is, those who really understood the present. I was a part of the larger action, in the U.S. Army in the field in China when the bombs were dropped. I could not comprehend what had happened, but I will never forget the moment when I got the information. We were in a convoy moving through a primitive, desolate area of western China when a rainstorm brought us to a halt, and we put up tents. I walked by an open tent and was hailed by a soldier who had just gotten the first report on a field radio.

Without any detail, we knew that the first bomb had changed the course of the war and our immediate lives. This was the subliminal message in the early reports. Soon we knew that Hiroshima and Nagasaki had been utterly destroyed and that the war, in effect, was over. We didn't know how long it would take the Japanese to comprehend this or whether the armies in China would surrender under any circumstance.

At that point I had no reservation about the destruction of life in the unimaginable holocausts. And, as response unfolded, we thought it remarkable that the argument of the bombs was so instantly effective. Within a relatively few days my group was airdropped into Nanking to participate in the surrender of the Japanese forces in China, Indochina, and Formosa. There had been no friendly forces in Nanking since the rape of the city some eleven years before. When we arrived, a hundred or so Americans, the city was entirely held and surrounded by fresh, heavily armed Japanese divisions. What an awesome chain of events was set off by those explosions.

In their immediate effect, the atom bombs were overwhelming. Our perception of this was delayed and selective, despite the fact that a complete report was made instantly available to the world. The totality of the event was immediately clear; the digestion of this staggering human disaster was an interminable process.

These are not the only events of this magnitude that we have had difficulty internalizing. We participated in what may have been an even greater act of violence in the firebombing of Dresden, Germany, an unarmed city. It is generally agreed today that Dresden should never have been attacked, but with the British and other Allies we attacked Dresden with incendiary bombs and started a fire storm that cremated virtually every living creature in the once beautiful city. The loss of life in Dresden was almost as great as the death toll in Hiroshima and Nagasaki combined. This episode was kept classified for many years and was, of course, officially lied about by our government. This was a matter of national security.

War efficiently produces all of the atrocities of which man is capable. When William Tecumseh Sherman said, "War is hell," he meant *hell* in the Old Testament sense. He didn't mean that it was unpleasant, but that it was the abode of evil—the most successful and respectable way of mass-producing violence that man has ever discovered. The only scourges that compete with war are plagues, earthquakes, floods, and other acts of God, but with his advanced technology man has gotten the upper hand. Now his obliterating explosions have the dividend of radiation; this is the ultimate violent reach of man.

While we are working our way through the megaviolence of World War II, we can look forward to the years it will take us to process Vietnam. Passing over particularly monstrous episodes like the illegal bombing of Cambodia, we can concentrate on the war proper—the bottom line of death and destruction. The unutterable violence that we laid on Vietnam for specious reasons is going to plague and dismay us for years to come. We dropped more millions of tons of bombs on this tiny rural nation than we did on all of Europe during World War II, and that whole destructive force is going to be visited on us. Every action brings an equal and opposite reaction: this is a moral as well as a physical law.

As a straight-arrow patriot, I was set up to be taken by the war in Vietnam. I was naturally violent and from a warlike people; we had fought in all of the wars from the Revolution on. World War II was a holy cause as far as I was concerned. Henry Luce and Franklin Roosevelt did the best they could, but they did not get us into the conflict soon enough. So, it took me a while on Vietnam.

As a reporter and an editor, I stood under a downspout of information for several years before I changed my mind. The reality of Vietnam began to dawn on me. Finally, when I realized how much I was being lied to, I decided that there could not be enough good sufficient truth anywhere there to justify what we were doing. It was a late conversion, and again this put me on both sides of one of the great questions of our time.

Truth is the message from reality, and without it we are lost. Unless we know what the reality is we have no way of knowing good from evil or right from wrong. A great violence done us directly during the Vietnamese War was the systematic denial of the truth. We as a people were lied to as a matter of high policy and simple expedience. If we had relied solely on our own government for information about the war, we would hardly have known that it existed. We would have had no recognizable description of our ally or our enemy, and we wouldn't have known where we were fighting or with what weapons. In the light of our history, how could we have placed such awesome confidence in our leaders?

Of course, it didn't last. The popular revolt against this war brought it to a seeming close. But it is *not* inoperative. We have to deal with it inside of ourselves, individually and collectively.

Only one thing is perfectly clear about Vietnam. The final end result on the ground will in no way resemble the goal or aim of any of our plans or strategies. We have not controlled the process. We can't shape the product. We will have about the same control of the ultimate destiny of Vietnam that the state has of the afterlife of the prisoner it executes. This experience has taught some of us, at least, that as a nation we can have really bad character.

It has taught us that political courses without proper goals become conspiracies against the truth and the right and the people—*us.*

It is extraordinary to me the way that America manages to produce a special anesthesia that deadens our feelings when we indulge in violence. We don't give this anesthesia to our victims to keep them from suffering; we take it ourselves. And, somehow, we make it through the suffering and pain that we inflict on others. This works for war and it works for peace. And there are certain aspects of our "domestic tranquillity" that are necessary to any consideration of our violence.

There seems to be an unquenchable propensity for *order* in our society. We have a passion for maintaining stable arrangements of people and ideas at all costs. This has long been true of not only our own conservatives but of persuasions across the political spectrum to fascism and beyond. It will never be forgotten that Mussolini made the trains run on time. And this not only makes the trains seem very late in Italy today, it is enough in the eyes of many to excuse Mussolini for everything else he did.

The last refuge of scoundrels may be the flag, but the last refuge of *the violent* is always *Law and Order.*

When you hear anybody invoking law and order, run like

hell. There is a kind of undifferentiated violence in this society that is dispersed under the label of law and order. As a political code phrase law and order has long since been broken and revealed to the world at large. Historically, it was a Southern phrase, and it meant *keeping the black folks down.* Nowadays it has been appropriated by the nation, and it has broader implications. The advocate may be against, not only blacks, who are a constant, but also demonstrators of all sorts for all causes —young people, hippies, streakers, the local minority, and any poor devils who run afoul of the no-knock laws, shakedown laws, and so on.

If you think of all of the force it takes to achieve perfect order, you will understand what the practical result is. **Order is violence, and absolute order is absolute violence.**

Maintaining law and order means a direct physical assault against anybody who may be technically standing on the wrong side of the law—not all laws, just those that have to do with maintaining perfect public order. Of course, anybody who raises questions about that order while it is being maintained is subject to the same law. Derelicts, scruffy-looking kids, long-haired rock-concert goers, blacks had all better be especially orderly, or they will get punched and clubbed and then arrested for disorderly conduct. To be *orderly* is to do and look the way I tell you, and that may be *not to be yourself.*

There is nothing theoretical about the way law enforcement works in the United States. We have to say at the start that it is selective, but law enforcement generally uses violence unless it is confronted by a stronger social, political, or physical force. For your own good, see that you possess one of these.

Back in the spring of 1973, there were some notorious examples. The perpetrators have since been charged, tried, and exonerated. The incident that riveted my attention took place in Collinsville, Illinois, and it involves a couple who were terroized by federal narcotics agents—*by mistake.* This is not an unusual occurrence or the most recent, but it has a lot to recommend it as an example. This sort of violence generally goes unnoticed because the victims are warned not to mention it by the very law they have to live under.

Herbert Giglotto and his wife, Evelyn, were asleep in their townhouse apartment in Collinsville, on a mild April night. Suddenly, there was a shattering crash as the front door was kicked in, and when Herbert stumbled from his bed, a gun was slapped against his head.

"One more step you son of a bitch and you're dead," a man snarled at him.

Fifteen long-haired, unshaven, armed men poured into the room, tearing it apart. While the men were ripping shelves out, dumping drawers, and wrenching clothes out of the closet, the leaders attended to Mr. and Mrs. Giglotto. They threw Herbert on the bed, face down, and handcuffed his arms behind his back. They flung his wife on the floor. "You move and you're dead. Who is this bitch?"

"That's my wife, and this is our bedroom!"

The federal agent cocked his pistol. "Don't get smart," he said. "I'm gonna kill you." From the floor where she lay in a short green nightie, Mrs. Giglotto pleaded hysterically for her husband's life. Obviously, they had been invaded by a motorcycle gang who was going to destroy the place first and then take care of them more deliberately, later.

They could hear the group breaking everything in the house that could be broken. Just as Herbert Giglotto was told that he would die if he didn't tell them where the drugs were, a voice came from the stairway. "We've made a mistake."

They had made a mistake, all right. Then they compounded it and proved their essential criminality. They knocked Giglotto down again, cursed him and his wife, and then left.

For a long time Mrs. Giglotto didn't even have the spirit to clean the place up. She couldn't sleep; she couldn't get the experience out of her mind. "Our things seem dirtied somehow, they aren't ours any more."[1]

Nobody knows how many innocent families have been assaulted by federal narcotics agents, with no known warrants. They are waging a vicious, sloppy sort of no-quarters war against drug dealers and folks that the good old boys in the bar down at the corner said "might be drug dealers." The incident is an outrage, but the really horrifying conclusion that you have to draw is that this is standard operating procedure for the narcs.

The quality of violence seems to be woven through our entire law enforcement mentality. Cops have never been able to understand that punishment is not their responsibility. As Don Imus, the morning disc jockey for WNBC, said half humorously, "Brutality is the fun part of law enforcement." If you study the way their police behave, you can understand the temperament of a people. The respectable citizens of any city in the United States would be aghast at the routine police brutality that goes on in their community. That is, the white citizens would be; the blacks wouldn't. The blacks have been trying to tell us for one hundred years how the cops have been treating them. Selective deafness and tunnel vision have helped us protect our composure.

It isn't safe to be black; it isn't even safe to be a black cop. Blacks are great targets, but brutality itself is not a matter of color. It is a matter of attitude. But if you have a choice, crack a black head. But remember when they had the police riot during the National Democratic Convention in Chicago? It was the little old man and his wife, Sarah, from Peoria who got clobbered by the cops. And it was their daughter Nancy who got her blouse and bra ripped off. And it was the great Mayor Daley who spat in the eye of the visiting dignitaries who protested.

I was there, and I saw it happen. Mobs are mobs, and it takes intelligence and cool to handle them—force too, sometimes. Any indecisiveness on the part of the authorities is disastrous. But charging the crowds in Chicago was not enforcement; it was assault. The cops had been building up fury all week under the greasy deluge of hippies, weirdos, radicals, beards, and good, clean-cut demonstrators from Dubuque; and they just blew. Bad law enforcement makes a very dangerous criminal. Rogue law enforcement is deadly. Together, they subvert the inherent decency of our system of government. It is especially ironic that government should harm people, that law and order should be one of our great sources of violence.

I know that this violence is a contagion in the arterial system of our society. We pass it from one to another like a disease. We do not protect each other in the streets of our cities; so we are unprotected ourselves. I feel the menace at night and the ill will at high noon. The last penalty of violence is that it distorts the human face of our fellowman, thereby taking away our own humanity. It takes away the possibility of the Good Samaritan in us, and, after all, everybody is traveling down the Jericho Road.

Just as all of life is made out of the same flesh, all of violence destroys life. And all violence is of a piece. Violence against other races, against other men's children, against women, against strangers and friends, violence against the earth itself— all of it is a seamless garment. It covers our lack of reverence for all living things.

What is the destructive instinct in us that makes us attack and despoil this fragile planet, spaceship earth? The establishment gets hysterical when the hippies trash-up beautiful Burbank. Yet, all the while their numberless factories are blowing trash into the sky and sluicing it off into our rivers. Our rivers are flush toilets. They are so toxic that they catch fire, and some of them are so putrid that we may have to bury them. You can walk on this water if you don't care what you step on.

We are just beginning to realize that everything has to be somewhere, that you can't throw anything away. One soft-drink bottle can live in the forests for a million years unless we recycle it. In our technological virtuosity we have even managed to leave garbage on the moon. And, on the way there, one of the astronauts lost his glove in space. For me the eternal symbol of clutter is the astronaut's glove; it will be there for millions of years. I can see it hanging there like a comic drawing of a hand, forefinger extended, pointing toward the cloud of pollution that covers Mother Earth.

There is no hiding place. Even the fish of the vasty deep are within the noxious cast of our poisons. We don't think much about the other living creatures that have to drink the water and breathe the air that we foul up. But somehow we have all got to live together. We have got to survive within the enchanted circle of the swordfish, the condor, the wharf rat, and the clam. It really takes more ancient eyes than ours to comprehend what we are doing to the skin and the air of our planet.

John Lansa, a Hopi elder, captures some of the profound concern of the Hopi Indians. From a deep spiritual sense of the delicate balance in nature, he speaks directly about the stripmining of Black Mesa and, by implication, about all of the violent damage we do to the earth.

"Before the white man came," Lansa says, "all the Hopi were happy and sang all the time. When the white man came, everything started to get out of balance. . . . The white brother has no spiritual knowledge, only technical."[2]

The white man does not have spiritual knowledge, but now he knows that he does not. He is sick of soul because he is beginning to see himself as he is. Our feeling of well-being as a nation has dried up so swiftly that it is almost like a death in the family. However people stand on the issues of the day, they stand together in thinking that life is almost too complicated to solve. If we can bear to look at society's failure to deal with international differences, to deal with the hunger and poverty of our own people, to deal with the destruction of urbanization, with every sort of crisis of conservation, if we confront these failures, we can see what hasn't worked.

We can't maintain order through violence. There are not cold mathematical solutions to any of these problems. We know they can't be solved with intellect or money. We can't get to the reality of any of these conditions unless we keep in touch with our feelings. Violence cuts that pathway off. We have got to approach our problems with love and understanding and concern in the light of their reality.

The vengefulness that we have seen in government, the hatred that has surfaced between the generations, the brutality behind law and order, the fury in all of the protestations—all of this has a common denominator. *Violence* is the name of everything that we as a people are reviewing and reconsidering now. This is not a remedy that works, but if we see violence where it exists and for what it is, we can come to a conclusion. It is not possible to commit violence with impunity. Any violence that we do is done to us.

There has been a national revulsion toward the war in Vietnam. The hatred between the generations has long since reached its high watermark and is subsiding. There has been a general swing of sentiment away from "the sanctity of business," the corruption of politics, the acceptance of war. We are becoming conscious and self-conscious about the tyranny of chauvinism. The old sense of sin is off its axis and shaking itself to pieces, but a new morality is being born.

I see violence in a new light, and I have stubbornly resisted broadening the definition. At times I have felt that I was being sucked through an underground river, lost as to direction. But now the confusion is clarified, and we have a sense of where events are taking us inside of our own minds. There is a new

American conscience emerging. Response from everywhere in our society brings fresh evidence. All of us are becoming sensitive to a broader spectrum of violence than we have ever been able to register before.

2

BUSINESS
Ethics and Idols

When I was a little kid, I couldn't imagine how I would ever make a living. Now I can't imagine how my children will. I am incorrigible when it comes to financial vision. This concern has survived the successes and failures of almost fifty years. I have always been a natural host for anxiety, but this is the only one I have been able to keep alive for so long. I must be the last of the depression babies—that great group of us that started out one jump ahead of starvation and has been scrambling to maintain that interval ever since.

Our psychology is that the economic footing is always slicker than it looks. You may think you've got your feet under you, but one misstep and you're on the skids. We weren't raised up in dire poverty; we were raised in apprehension. It was the anxiety of the Great Depression that turned us all into hungry fighters. There was a quality of ill-being in the air that got into our bones and encouraged us to have curious notions about money and business. Actually, in my family there was never any agonizing about finances, but money was the everlasting unspoken word.

My dad didn't need to say a thing about the demands of his job. The tenor of family life told me, in all sort of ways, that his

business was full of strain and uncertainty and that his management of it was worthy of respect. In those uncertain days you
had to be lucky and indispensable. Father understood the problems and impositions of business the way an Oriental under-
stands fate. Many years ago, early in the depression, he would
come home at night through the pine trees, and from his expression and his walk came signs of weariness and tension. A
child smells every emotion that a familiar adult carries with
him, and I would shake him down in a split second.

He had no guile, no side, as is sometimes the case with people
of great innocence who are unafraid. His face told me about the
day. I frequently got the feeling that it had not thrown him but
that he had not thrown it. I knew how intelligent and strong he
was; so I surmised that if he couldn't throw it, it must be some
contest. It was, and it went on forever.

My old man had no recklessness, but he left his corporation
and founded his own company. I understand this since I have
done the same thing. But at the low point of the depression he
sold his company to his old corporation and went back to work
for them as a salesman. I have often thought that he was the
most unlikely entrepreneur I have ever known. But then I will
have to admit that he was no stereotype of a salesman either.

There was a long period of time there in the South when
people's lives were tossed all over the place. Businessmen lost
their jobs, and they did whatever they could; some pumped gas
—there was plenty of it and it was cheap. There were a lot of
confused and bruised feelings, and while people were doing
what they could to stay alive, they were trying to figure out new
identities. A lot of them never made it. Naturally, we kids got
the feeling through our pores that if you didn't scramble you
might very well starve to death. It was root hog or die. So we
sure didn't grow up laughing at business or at businessmen. The
luxury of that was a long way down the road.

My father was always talking about my learning a trade,

something that I could fall back on if my job collapsed. He expected the depression to come back. He was set to give the alarm. "Watch out! Here it comes again." If it hit us again he wanted me to be protected. But the point is he thought that any individual was likely to have to make an extraordinary effort to survive economically. He personally was determined to survive. He passed along to me a set of attitudes he had about something he called "the company." It was his code of ethics about his own work.

The Company was sort of like the country: it was run by good and bad people, but it was due loyalty and devotion. It had a preferred and protected position among the institutions of our lives, and it was our company right or wrong. The job was sacrosanct. It was unthinkable that the job would not be done properly, no matter what the cost in hours or bone marrow or anything else. Without really being aware of it, I accepted all of these values. My father put his work ahead of his family, his pleasure, and his health; that's the way it was. It was a matter of being true to himself; he was not trying to please anybody. He was never afraid of any superiors or cared particularly what they thought of him.

This was a pretty stern code, and it depended on *character,* a word that he admired. He was an old-fashioned gentleman, and I think, in many ways, I became an old-fashioned little boy. My father would have agreed with the idea that we are never closer to reality than when we are working. And thinking back about the content of his life, his most satisfying times came after he had done what he called *a good job.* He understated everything.

It didn't occur to me for many years that I had gotten my perfectionism from him. I also got his addiction to work; I got hooked on the Protestant Work Ethic. If he had been pleasure bent, I might have grown up as a lazy, fun-loving Southern Presbyterian and had myself a helluva good time.

Now that I see the process in perspective, part of it is pretty funny. Without knowing it, he was converting me, after his own image, into the most dangerous sort of employee in the world. He was busy teaching me how to be *a hard-working, incorruptible man*. This sort of man can ruin any business, wreck any corporation. Many times in the last few years I've thought I'd like to retrace his steps. I'm sure his wake was strewn with mangled conspiracies, disrupted takeover plans, busted signals, and exposed chicanery. What a way to go.

When the time came, I was loaded with this odd sort of moral armor and had no idea where the action was. He had not only made me unacceptable to business; he had also neglected to tell me where it was located and what it was all about. I think it was a common experience for my generation to find at the outset that the business world seemed mysterious and impenetrable. This is one reason so many of my classmates went on to graduate school; they couldn't bear to jump in. But ultimately most of us have got to get connected.

After all, everybody's got to be somewhere. There is no choice, but also there is a terrible yearning in most human beings to belong to something, no matter what it is. The average man is walking around in no-man's-land, lonely and miserable, trying to find somebody to surrender to. Independence is isolation; freedom is confusion; choice is bewilderment. Since we do not have a totalitarian state, an awesome responsibility falls on business. Business has to take this surrender and give this pilgrim a hitch for his loyalty, a cause for his devotion, an identification tag. He's got to be able to tell anybody at the crossroads, "I sell for Shell," or "I cure hams for ITT." Since it is what a person does that gives him identity, not what he is, he can't get into the other man's computer without the essential piece of programming: "I do so-and-so."

Man has a tropistic instinct to join a group just as a newborn holds close to a human presence. It is absolutely amazing how an employee will attribute the basic, sustaining *human* characteristics to a corporation. This sort of anthropomorphism simulates something very close kin to romantic love—unrequited, that is. It is a self-completing sort of involvement that allows an employee to unload love, devotion, and loyalty and feel the indispensable vassal to the mighty king. Like romantic love, it does not always require anything very definite in return.

Business in the United States is not just business; it is a political party, a social club, a tribe; it is the *means* to the great American *end*, success. If you have what we call ambition, that is, a desire to better yourself, you almost have to subscribe to business. Getting ahead in business is an ideal built into the most basic human aspirations in our society. The self-made man makes it all the way in business, the implication being from the bottom up and with the tactics of the jungle. This jungle warfare in somebody's background is okay; it is almost admired. When the lid is blown off the business scene by some explosion like Watergate, a certain number of economic knife-fighters are revealed to be intimately connected at the top of government. Blue ribbon society may not accept them, but top business does. Business is not critical.

Our free enterprise system was not mentioned in the Constitution, but it is the most powerful covenant that we have. In its purest form it is cutthroat competition, the only legal sort of dueling that we have around today. In its most exalted form, it operates on a multinational basis and controls governments, national economies, and everything else. The major oil companies have proven that they feed most sumptuously when the supply is short, the price is high, and the general economy is shaky. Business American style is a sort of institutionalized violence that we have become oblivious to, and its pursuit deadens the conscience of the practitioner. We do damage to people in business even if we play according to the rules. And the rules are not that well enforced.

More directly, profit and loss are the good and evil of business, and the bottom line is the end. Almost all means are justified by it. If you can believe that what is good for General Motors is good for America, then you can graduate to the suspension of disbelief about ITT. Of course there is the assumption that your welfare is bound with the welfare of dozens of nations with no common denominator except ITT.

The Roman Empire lasted for nine hundred years not just because of its military might, which it had, but because it ruled people's minds. It governed inside of the head with a grip that was well-nigh unbreakable. American business has the same secret of government. Business is an empire that has its topless towers, its fleets, its panoply and pomp, but mostly it rules invisibly, inside of the wants and needs of prime ministers and kings and sheiks and ordinary folks. The universal language is greed, and business speaks it fluently. It is more widely understood than loyalty or fear. Business operates in an expanding market of this appetite. It relies on the fact that the compulsion for things is never satisfied. The greedy man or nation is like the gambler, the nymphomaniac, the alcoholic, all of whom are intoxicated with the process—staying forever at the brink. With these compulsions the *means* are the only *end* there is.

We have always felt more beholden to business than we have to sex or God. We have understood it better and have been more comfortable with it. Our awe, ecstasy, fear, and exultation have come in business and not in bed or in church. However, business gets into bed with us frequently and goes to church with us every Sunday. As Otto Bremer puts it in an article in the Harvard Business Review: "Business is today the most significant force shaping American life and the strongest influence determining the everyday values of the average citizen; the operative values in the management of a corporate enterprise tend to become the operative values in the daily life of society."[1]

Of course this is reflected in the basic social unit, the family. Bremer talks about this with some dismay. "In my marriage and family counseling," he says, "I often encounter people who look upon the family as primarily a financial institution. . . . Unconditional love, in the traditional, religious sense, has given way in these families to the standards of accountability appropriate to business."[2] In discussing divorce, rejection of the young, and other difficulties with these people, he discovers that these problems frequently have their roots in the charge that someone is "unproductive" or "does not contribute to the family success."

Family success in human terms is the result of intimate, creative contributions among the members. It comes from a sort of reckless willingness to do the right thing by each other. Very often what works and what is right are different. People can be admired for costly *right* judgments; businesses, never. When business picks what's right and rejects what works, it confounds its own processes. The advantage of the family is that it is nonprofit, and it can take infinite pains with its individual members. Business can do violence to its employees, to other businesses, to the fragile world that we live in, but it may not fail to make a profit. In short, business can *treat people like things,* and within its own logic, it must if this is what it takes to do business.

It would seem that man's spiritual values would conflict with the methods of business. The biblical injunction is very clear. Jesus said, "How hard it is for rich people to enter the Kingdom of God! It is much harder for a rich man to enter the Kingdom of God than for a camel to go through the eye of a needle." Businessmen certainly don't have any problem entering church. As a matter of fact, as far as we know, business has not taken over heaven, but it has most certainly taken over the churches. The biggest crisis in most churches every year is making the budget. And certainly one of the greatest budgetal priorities is maintaining the plant. The church's treasures would seem to be largely in terrestrial holdings presided over by businessmen.

Businessmen support the church; they run it as lay members. And they have been in charge during the successive decades of this century while the church was keeping its distance from the most critical social problems. It was bad business to worry about the hideous living and working conditions of mill workers and immigrants early in the century, and the church, by and large, did not. The denominations and councils have made honest efforts now and then. They condemned Vietnam and demanded civil rights for the blacks and justice for those shot at Kent State; they extolled Martin Luther King, Jr., and tried to help Angela Davis. But, not with impunity. The businessmen cut their allowances off, attacked them through media, and trimmed them back to size.

Just as the majority of churchmen in the South refused to take any role in desegregating the Southern cities, or the Southern churches, for that matter, the Northern businessmen, twenty years later, refuse to let the churches in the comfortable little suburbs condemn our role in Vietnam or speak up for amnesty. It is the same infusion of the business ethic and the masterly knack of keeping theology out of the practice of religion. It is selective perception that does not challenge the mindset. It has also been a chauvinistic, masculine influence that has kept the church from becoming any kinder, any more forgiving, any more sensitive to the needs of surrounding human beings.

Don't knock it. If you knock business in our society, you are knocking America and God. It's blasphemous to kick the golden calf or to disparage his habitat, the free enterprise system. Somehow we got this little bit of idolatry going good, and although we still pay lip service to God, our strength and our daily bread come from ITT or GM or Exxon. Business is our religion. Today, with the multinational corporations and the conglomerates, American business passes understanding. In a sense, the church is a sort of wholly owned subsidiary. And it is fairly easy to see how it got that way.

It is true that early in the century conscience was struck and responded to the charges against the robber barons, that there were cries of moral indignation about the virtual imprisonment of employees and the abandonment of the poor. But, confronting this thin line of Christian critics were redoubtable men of God who had somehow gotten a taste for Mammon. They were prodigal in laying God's approval and his special blessings on the rich and mighty. Bishop William Lawrence of Massachusetts wrote in 1901 that man could recognize two guiding principles in his life. "First, that it is his divine mission to conquer Nature, open up her resources, and harness them to his service. The second is that in the long run, it is only to the man of morality that wealth comes, for Godliness is in league with riches."[3]

The *morality* that the bishop is talking about is antithetical to the concern of the New Testament. Jesus felt so strongly about wealth because the *process* of accumulating it had proved to be so destructive. We call that process *business.* It is right to make money in business and wrong not to; profit is good and loss is bad.

Honesty, generosity, and truthfulness in business are reckless experiments. They stand in the way of good business practice on every level. Some businesses are daring enough to stand behind these excesses, and some individuals are dauntless enough to engage in them; but from a corporate point of view, this would be aberrant or temporary insanity. An executive known to be literally honest may be gently disqualified from handling a given part of any company's business. Through unspoken agreement, certain executives are not to speak to certain customers or participate in certain deals. Incorruptible men are scattered throughout all of business, but they are forever colliding with plans, policies, and human beings bent on mischief.

Great crises always throw light on curious corporate behavior, and we are indebted to the energy crisis for a number of illuminating revelations. In early 1974, Justice Hyman Korn of the State Supreme Court of New York was questioning the Royal Dutch Shell family about the *shell game* they had been playing with wholesalers. One Shell company, Asiatic Petroleum, had bought a million barrels of oil from an overseas sister company back in '73. Since it was imported, this oil was free of controls. After the October war in the Middle East and the onset of the energy crisis, Asiatic brought out this imported oil and made a killing on it—47.5 cents a gallon (what the market would bear).

The upshot was that while Shell-U.S.A. was selling wholesalers at 14 cents a gallon, those wholesalers dependent on Asiatic were paying 47.5 cents a gallon the same month. Dismayed by this inequity, Justice Korn asked the attorney for Shell why Asiatic had done this, what was the motive?

"I guess to make money," a Mr. Harold McGuire answered.

"So does a fellow who goes out in the street with a gun do it to make money," Justice Korn replied. "But you have to have a moral. You can't do it on the backs of people."[4]

Business morality is always a surprise to the young initiates who graduate from college every year. Buckminster Fuller, engineer, philosopher, inventor, says, "So we got a large crop of young people coming into the corporations under the impression that you could do the job and be moral. They were cruelly disenchanted. But now, among the administrations of those vast companies, I find a beautiful bunch of men who would really like to do things in a fantastically moral way. But they've inherited the momentum of these corrupt practices, and there isn't much they can do about it." Fuller adds, "The idea that a corporation has any morality is entirely wrong. They were developed with the idea of limited liability, and it has permeated all their thinking. So they also limit their morality."[5]

The morality of business would depend in part on its view of its own employees. Does business encourage the sort of individuality that supports good moral behavior and independent moral judgments of executives and workers? Since the influence does not seem to be in this direction, what do corporate attitudes about man reveal about corporations? It is not possible to go beyond a few generalizations which are more comment than definition, but certain responses are predictable.

Too much intelligence or sensibility ill fits a person for business which depends on simplifying, not complicating. Business cannot allow many exceptions. It must subject everything it does to relatively crude systems that fit no individual case perfectly. Every creative effort is an uncomfortable experience for businessmen whose whole confidence lies in replicating or mass-producing and not creating. Business distrusts, dislikes, and systematically exploits creative people and any work that they do. The degree of hostility varies enormously, but exceptions to this general attitude are rare indeed.

Every time man repeats himself, he suffers and business benefits. All sales spiels are standardized and memorized; all screws are twisted in clockwise; all reports are made in triplicate. And so would all satisfactory employees be made in triplicate were that possible. Business does not want new and different people; it wants more of the same sort of productive, dependable people that it already has. If cloning becomes inexpensive and reasonably dependable, endless copies of standard, efficient company men will be created. Nobody with unrelenting moral standards would be copied; no master politicians would be copied either.

Robert Townsend,[6] a sort of Voltaire of the American business world, talks about his years as an executive at American Express. "During those years (1948–62)," he says, "the company was rich enough to do—and did—almost everything wrong. In that near-perfect learning environment I formed the valuable habit of observing what action was taken, considering the *opposite* course, and then working back, when necessary, to what really made sense."[7]

Townsend likes to quote John Ise, the Kansas radical, who said, "The modern corporation is a legal individual without an ass to kick or a soul to save."[8] An understanding of this definition would save many a derailed businessman from the futile effort of trying to punish or convert his corporation.

Wherein we are not governed by business we are governed by politics. Not surprisingly, the moral blindness and natal avarice of business have found a comfortable, permanent home in the body politic. You can hardly be better buddies than business and politics have become. Most of the great political problems have involved managing the investments of business. During the early '70s American business virtually ran the national political machine. And the text is Watergate and its collateral connections.

Just as the bottom line in business is profits, in politics it is election to office. In both disciplines the positive result is to be achieved at any cost. Business and politics make love with a smooth line about prosperity, but they want to do what everybody else wants to do who makes love, and they usually succeed. If anything, the politician's courtship appeals to even more primitive instincts. People will vote for people to do things for them that they wouldn't do for themselves in any way, shape, or form.

In the political game you follow a trail of unmarked one-hundred-dollar bills, and every one of them was earned by some businessman somewhere, and each bill was given in exchange for preferential treatment. The great excuse for Watergate was that corporate espionage has been going on forever and is an accepted practice; business offered the example, but, unfortunately, politics bungled the techniques. The kindest explanation of the behavior of the White House staff during the pre-Watergate Nixon administration was that the assistants to the president were acting out of blind loyalty, not thinking for themselves. This is the way of life over at the corporation.

It is interesting to note that both business and politics sell unreality. Both are interested in the efficacy of the *sell* and not the product. The marketing man is king in business now, and as soon as he speaks, you can recognize him. He talks about the particularities of the *sell* and of *distribution;* he hardly mentions the product except for packaging. Marketing's greatest recent success was the packaging of Richard Nixon. Once the product has been accepted by the consumer, it doesn't matter what happens to it. However, the question of truth in advertising has come up. And the ground rules are going to change, but slowly.

Once you accept "person as thing," then the next step is "person as product." We have highly refined techniques for mass-marketing products. Of course, this whole process is blasphemous, and our consciousness is very gradually being raised about it. The corrections will come in politics first; it will be fascinating to see if they affect the conduct of business—how much, how soon.

If people are things, and/or products, then it is not hard to think of the living earth as being no more than a food bin or root cellar. If anything you want is down there, get it. Animal, vegetable, and mineral wealth comes from the earth, and we have rapaciously taken it from earliest times, usually heedless of the damage or the waste. It is interesting that the oil companies, the stars of the energy crisis, enjoy the greatest profits ever made in the history of business. They got their product from way down in the earth, and it's been in the process of being created by the earth itself for forty-four million years. At least mythically, it belongs to all of us.

With a multinational leverage and captive administrations, business has an awesome power to rip off the helpless consumer. If they cripple their own competition in the process, well, c'est la guerre. Who would think that government and business would get together to destroy the freedom of enterprise?

Somehow, long ago, business got a franchise to take over the territory, America, and develop it anyway they wanted to. Finally, the ecological movement is trying to flag this juggernaut down. "Save the birds and animals; don't tear the skin off the earth; save the swamps; save the rivers and the lakes; spare the air," and so it goes until what's endangered gets to be a catalog of everything we have on this nice, warm planet Earth. In the past, we've seen business willing to process human beings along with materials, that is, expose them to damaging dust, chemicals, and gases that change them permanently. So we shouldn't expect too much mercy for the landscape, seascape, or random critters.

Occasionally there is an iconic utterance by business that captures perspective, and we'd better learn what it looks like from that vantage point if we're going to make it down here. Charles Luce, chairman of the board of Consolidated Edison, discussed the substitution of coal for oil in creating energy. "Well," Luce said, "It's a question of how much clean air we can afford."[9]

It's really a question of how much Con Ed we can afford; being hooked on Con Ed is bad business. You get so you enjoy living better electrically, and then the cost soars. Suddenly you've got a habit you can't support. We've all listened to the barker and come into the electric circus; suddenly the good stuff gives out, and they start bringing in the cheap stuff. Sixteen tons and what do you get? A little slow of breath and deeper in debt.

Finally, as we get our second wind we began to have some

second thoughts about the free enterprise system as it works on the ground. It's hard to knock it in terms of profit and loss, but it's not very good theology. I can't say that I haven't been touched by greed to the point of pixilation a few times, but my consciousness has been raised lately. I am trying to turn over a new life.

I speak of business the way an AA speaks of booze—from inside of the arrangement. I have been hooked, and now that I am off of it, I am okay, day by day. There is no guarantee that I won't relapse and go back some day. I can't pass an underwriter without bending double with greed. But I know I can't go public day after tomorrow. And I know that if the market improves, next month, or whenever, it won't happen for me then either. I'll never be cured, but for the time being I am recovered. The needs of the day are sufficient unto the day.

It is the irony of reality that, finally, your whole fortune has got to be inside of you while the process of business, absolutely insures that it will be outside of you. It is the *process* that you have to live with, that has to satisfy your soul. Just as surely as Faust did, you make a contract with the Devil when you do it for the *end*. And the Devil doesn't care whether you believe in him or not. He doesn't even have to exist to collect.

In the past we have been just as simple minded about business as we have been about sex. In effect we have said that work was good and that sex was bad. Now the prophets are saying that work is bad and sex is good—a total reversal. These jolting times have shaken loose the young from the addictions of the older generations, and they have been experimenting, critically, with both sex and work. They find that neither is either, that is, necessarily good or bad. But the intrinsic value of work has lost it narcotic power, and the young have flatly rejected the old ethic that idleness is evil and work is good.

The ancients would have had no truck with the Protestant Work Ethic. Aristotle wrote, "Leisure is the first principle of all action and so leisure is better than work and is its end." This obsession with work is a fairly new and tacky phenomenon in the history of man. But during its vogue, it has been total, especially in America.

On all levels of society we are coming out of a long period of bondage. We know that our work has proved to be more addictive than all of the poisonous drugs and chemicals ever invented by man. Business has been a narcotic, and like certain other narcotics it is so dangerous because we have a tremendous tolerance for it. It takes more and more of the fruits of business to satisfy us, and as we build the habit, our dependency grows, and we lose contact with the rest of life. We also lose touch with our own emotions and the wisdom of our hearts. Those who are completely absorbed by work live entirely intellectually, just as alcoholics do. Our consciousness has been raised about all of this, and we are coming unbound.

It is astonishing how the old sense of sin failed to register the exploitation of men, women, and children who powered the industrialization of this country. As individuals, we have been insensitive to and unaware of the routine destruction of human values and environment resulting from the rampageous growth of business and industry. We have failed to temper public and private greed with concern for all aspects of the future, for physical and spiritual preservation.

Diverse elements in the national work force have spontaneously come to life with new awarenesses. Blue-collar workers in the mass-production industries are rebelling against jobs that use only a small part of them, that mutilate them and prevent them from being whole people. There is deep and widespread restlessness among white collar groups in dozens of major industries. And young people are raising profound questions about materialism that puts work in a new perspective. This generation has taken a step back and looked out of their eyes differently at business.

Young people don't believe that work is sacred, and they do not believe it is divisible from leisure or play. They have given all sorts of signs that they are aware of the necessity of keeping in touch with the mythic, the spiritual, and primitive instincts that allow them to have complex emotional lives, that keep them in touch with the magic of the past. They suspect that material things do not bring happiness, that if you give your heart to things, you will lose your soul. There is a universal appreciation among the young of what they mean when they say, "Mr. Businessman." There is a whole different perception.

When they walk away from the obvious, sequential steps to a secure future, is it because they don't even understand what the word *security* means to us? Are they blowing the future, or do they understand the present better than we do? Are they released from the myth that has become a monster: If you work hard and subordinate yourself to your job, there will be a great reward. A payday. I don't know, and they don't entirely know.

They do know this: *Greed* kills just like *speed.*

We didn't lose Eden or Camelot; we threw them away when we went into a joint venture with some snake or other. Once we have demythologized work, we can look at all aspects of it more clearly. We have broken through to a new reality about business. We are beginning to see the mysterious workings of the free enterprise system one frame at a time. It stops the action when a friendly tycoon like Mr. Luce asks, "How much clean air can we afford?" Our innocence is gone. Our eyes are open. We can no longer deny the effect that our idolatrous devotion to material success has on spiritual values.

There will be a new American conscience about the behavior of companies and corporations. We are at a new reality in understanding the role of the individual in business. Certainly we will be freed from the old sense of sin that we have had about leisure, but we will be burdened with concerns about all aspects of the conduct of our nation's business. The postindustrial era will have a different moral climate.

We are still processing the whole impact of the Industrial Revolution. But the insights that we are having now will profoundly affect our future judgments of what is good and what is evil.

3

POLITICS

Witness and False Witness

You grow up in the briar patch of politics if you are raised in the South. It's dense and prickly, but it's home. Since a surprising number of Southerners are related or acquainted, politicians never succeed in being remote. Of course, it would be political suicide, but it is also socially impossible. Southerners know that they elect some rascals for term after term, but they are their rascals. They are also enormously responsive to the governed in a personal way. Political leaders get drunk and have to be hauled about by the state patrol, or they tomcat around and the word gets out, but they are not very strong on the cold vices. My experience is that politicians down home do some very unusual things, but they never really surprise anybody.

We are not surprised when a governor has a four-lane highway built up to his milk barn. Convenience must be served. We weren't too surprised in Georgia when we turned up with two governors at the same time, and it looked like we might have three. In the South we have had hillbilly singers as governors; we've had governors who converted their capitols into frenzied activity on the few days a month that they were sober and could sign bills. We've had governors who dated burlesque queens and governors who routinely seduced ladies in elevators, or anywhere else with reasonable privacy. There has been a tradition of allowing a certain amount of idiosyncrasy, if never arrogance. We expect a man to breathe.

I will never forget the campaigns of Eugene (Gene) Talmadge, the father of Herman Talmadge, senior senator from Georgia. They say that Gene had fires in his belly, and he certainly had sparks in his eyes. He also grazed a cow on the lawn of the governor's mansion in Atlanta. Some years ago he was campaigning against Jimmy Carmichael, a formidable moderate, and Gene said: *"Comical* is against the boll weevil and for fair weather. His campaign is like a Mother Hubbard—it covers everything and touches nothing." Gene would take his front teeth out when he was talking to farmers and put them back in again before he spoke to the trustees of the University of Georgia. He spoke well either way.

There is a much-loved story about Gene Talmadge and an old farmer whose son was in the state prison. The man had come to beg the governor to pardon his boy. During a lull in the conversation, Talmadge's eyes flicked out across a nearby pasture.

"Hey, see that old cow there," he said.

"Yup."

"How'd you like to buy that cow for $2500?"

The old man gasped, "What in the world would I need a $2500 cow for?"

"Well," Talmadge said reflectively, "your boy has got to have something to ride home from the penitentiary."

Gene is long since dead and gone, and gone with him is the old South and all of old RFD America. But the present is connected to the past in more ways than one. Herman Talmadge, Gene's son, was on the Senate Watergate Committee—my own spiritual representative. The father and son span my memory of politics. I have been on a long journey, all the way from the old days of the poll tax and the white primary to bugging, burglary, and executive privilege. Incidentally, we have in our national politics moved from the warm vices to the cold vices. It is easy for me to understand how Herman Talmadge is filtering this whole Watergate thing through his mind because, in a sense, we have made this trip together.

Today, politics is less colorful, less attractive, but much more preposterous than anything I have ever known of or heard about. Watergate brought us full circle, back to the starting point of our Republic. Voices of our founders right out of the American Revolution have come into the national dialogue. Thomas Jefferson's name has been invoked, and his ghost has come thumping up through the floorboards, and Thomas Paine seems to be addressing himself directly to what has been going on under our eyes. In tracing our origins and the intent of our founding documents, we have come face to face with our founders, arguing over the same issues that divided and united them. Such agonizing questions have been raised, questions that are so deeply constitutional that we have had to struggle to understand how we came about in the first place.

After almost two hundred years, the American Revolution is still working through our consciousness. This was an astonishing event because it was almost unthinkable that a republic would work; historically, there was little justification for this leap of faith. As today, the standing prejudices in the conservative minds were against revolution, against freedom, against letting the common man govern. There was an almost universal constraint against breaking the ties with Britain.

After several major battles with the British, George Washington stoutly maintained that he was fighting the colonial governors and not the king. As a matter of fact, he was still toasting George III in officers' mess. In retrospect, the really crucial battle was the struggle to win the continental mind. Somehow, the people had to be persuaded that a perilous and uncertain independence was preferable to security through dependence on England. This is all relevant today.

The Watergate imbroglio showed us that freedom is as beleaguered as ever, and the principles set forth in the Declaration of Independence and in the Constitution have been stirred to the surface of our consciousness by the events of this day. We have not outgrown the Constitution; we have not grown up to it yet. And the Declaration of Independence that gave us our spiritual freedom and our sense of nation still has the pulse and fragility of life itself. The original energy is not spent.

The Declaration of Independence is no ordinary document. It prefigured concepts of government that are still evolving into reality almost two hundred years later. This declaration came out of a leadership that was no more miraculous than it was providential. We couldn't begin to produce the quality of the Continental Congress today with seventy times the population that we had in colonial days. Once when the Nobel laureates gathered for a reception, President John Kennedy said slyly that there hadn't been that much intelligence in the White House since Thomas Jefferson had supper by himself before the fire in his study. Well, Jefferson finished the first draft of the Declaration of Independence on June 28, 1776, and the world has not been the same since.

In its finished form the declaration became a radical, fateful, and contagious document that changed the way man thought. The preamble recognizes the divine spark and reflects a changed concept of man. It begins: "We hold these truths to be self-evident, that all men are created equal, that they are endowed by their Creator with certain unalienable Rights, that among these are Life, Liberty and the pursuit of Happiness." As familiar as this assertion is, it makes the hairs prickle up on your neck when you read it aloud. And in the context of its own time, the ideas were stunning.

Distinguished American historian Samuel Eliot Morison

writes: "These words are more revolutionary than anything written by Robespierre, Marx or Lenin."[1]

The declaration, the Constitution, the Revolutionary War did not just come about inevitably. As always, independence started with an independence of mind, an emblazoned sort of insight into the condition of man, and an assumption of the responsibility for doing something about it. The elements in this singular bridge in human history are curiously reminiscent of events in recent history. Britain provided the crises, that in accumulation broke through to new perspectives of human freedom, to a great new reality. The catalyst in this situation was a journalist, Thomas Paine.

It is interesting that in our time when freedom was under great stress, a few inspired journalists working for a handful of redoubtable newspapers have made a contribution of the same kind, if not the same moment, that Paine made. Paine's whole progress, the electrifying position that he took, the galvanic force of his communication, and the outcry against freedom of expression, all of this has an unsettling relevance. The way the continental mind responded to Paine's writing and the way his concepts worked through the consciousness of his time were as important to the founding of our nation as the working of these same principles are to its maintenance today.

Bear in mind that Tom Paine named us the United States of America; he inspired our Declaration of Independence and was in a very real sense the godfather of our nation. His book, *Common Sense,* turned George Washington around in his tracks and convinced him that severing connections with Britain was a fateful necessity. Paine urged the colonies to take up arms against the British. He wrote: "The sun never shined on a cause of greater worth. Tis not the affair of a city, a county, a province, or a kingdom; but of a Continent—of at least one eighth part of the habitable globe. Tis not the concern of a day, a year or an age; posterity are virtually involved in the contest, and will be more or less affected even to the end of time, by the proceedings now."[2]

This same man was profoundly suspicious of government: "Society is produced by our wants," he wrote, "and government by our wickedness. . . . Society in every state is a blessing, but government even in its best state, is but a necessary evil; in its worst state an intolerable one."[3]

And Paine asked rhetorically, "But where, say some, is the king of America?" And then as if he were speaking out of a vision, ". . . in America, the law is king. For as in absolute governments the king is law, so in free countries the law ought to be king; and there ought to be no other."[4]

As we look back on President Nixon's isolation from Congress, from the people, and from the writings of journalists like Paine, we can see a condition that Paine associated with monarchy. "There is something exceedingly ridiculous in the composition of monarchy," he wrote in *Common Sense*, "it first excludes a man from the means of information, yet empowers him to act in cases where the highest judgment is required. The state of a king shuts him from the world, yet the business of a king requires him to know it thoroughly; wherefore the different parts, by naturally opposing and destroying each other, prove the whole character to be absurd and useless."[5]

Paine saw the law as being the very definition of a democratic form of government. Within the sort of government that he envisioned, it would have been unthinkable to Paine for an American president to set himself above the law and organize an invasion of constitutional privacy and protection. And to say that it was done in the name of national security, he understood this ruse. The technique of destroying freedom in the name of national security was the most common weapon of his enemies, the Federalists.

Tom would have laughed himself silly at the idea of protecting America from revolutionary elements. He was a revolutionary element, and so were Washington and Jefferson and Franklin and on and on. If Paine had not been a revolutionary, we might not have become a nation.

Two hundred years after the American Revolution, we are still processing the events of our founding. We are still fighting about the protection that our Constitution gives the individual citizen. And during one fateful interval along the way, the Civil War, we came close to losing our concept of nation and a good bit of its geography. Unless you are a Southerner or a historian, it is hard to conceive of the psychological, economic, and cultural traumas caused by the greatest war the world had known up to that time. The Civil War was the realization of the worst fears that the colonials had about the vulnerability of a republic.

Now the rebels were Southerners and not colonials, and the war utterly destroyed the old political and moral landscape. Economic and psychological effects of it are still alive, and the folk memory of a substantial part of our total population includes being a vanquished people. It is extraordinary to remember that the countryside was ravaged, the towns were sacked and burned, and a whole way of life—that included slavery— was wiped out. And, of course, instead of getting massive economic relief as the Japanese and the Germans did, the South was occupied and garrisoned through the vengeful years of Reconstruction.

As a Southerner, this experience is not remote; it is immediate. I know what family silver was stolen, what damage the deserters and bushwhackers did, and I know the houses that Sherman burned, and those that escaped. My great-great-grandmother was forced to leave Atlanta in an open boxcar with two children sick with scarlet fever in her arms. This Iliad was imprinted on my mind as a tiny child. I know that I am the first generation that does not at least in some metaphorical way think of the North as the enemy. My mother's eyes burn when she tells old stories of how the Yankee soldiers took the silver, burned the homes, and sassed the ladies—and ruined the old kingdom for good.

The lost cause is a powerful piece of mythology, and it can generate fierce, distorted attitudes. Losing a war is much more instructive than winning, and it does strange things to the psychology of a people. The most fascinating example is Palestine. Before the first century, that little country had been conquered by the Romans, the Babylonians, the Assyrians, twice by the Egyptians, by the Greeks, the kings of Antioch, and the Persians. The Palestinians were more incendiary at the end of this two thousand years than they were at the beginning, and took on Rome again. The South didn't go quite this far, but she developed a ferocious identity, a certain amount of paranoia, a fine sense of irony, and a complex, phantasmagoric consciousness.

The Republican party was despised in the South and this antagonism maintained long enough to create all sorts of paradoxical political configurations. With the sort of folk memory the South had, you'd never think that the region would go Republican. It took generations of new wealth, and an influx of new population, not to speak of industrial development, and *time*. Of course, greed was the agent of reconciliation; it is the universal solvent. If you understand this little dynamic, you can understand political loyalty that blinks at everything. This has helped me understand some die-hard support of Nixon's role in Watergate.

A man's affection is never diverted from the party that protects his pocketbook. If they also happen to agree about law and order, that is, who should be punished, it's a permanent seal. I guess it's as simple as this: when people and regions begin to get prosperous, the consumption of Scotch goes up, and the sense of history diminishes. But sufficient crisis can overturn this mindset and open the view to a new reality.

I am still trying to understand the after-effects of the Civil War. Some of the fallout has been working its way through the

Southern consciousness ever since and is just beginning to surface. The freeing of the slaves was an overwhelming experience. Not only were the blacks freed, but the whites slowly began to be free of the old ways of seeing them. Slowly, but inexorably, the humanity of the Negroes began to penetrate the awareness of the whites. This process is continuous. No moderate or conservative white Southerner of our time would have said, in 1960, that he felt great guilt about the treatment of the blacks. He might have been sincerely sorry about the inequities and the suppression, but he was not aware of any personal guilt.

I rejected the idea that I should feel guilty for anything as complex and incomprehensible as the black odyssey in the South. I wouldn't accept any piece of any collective guilt, and I thought this bit of ideology was untenable. However, all this time, my own conscience was grappling with other failures that had nothing to do with any collective anything. I realize now that I personally failed to understand the black person's struggle, the impossible psychic cost to him of just existing. Life was rigged against him. He couldn't live a self-respecting life. This may seem self-evident, but it has taken a while for us to internalize it. Now, for the first time I have a feeling of the immensity of the human problems that were at stake in the Civil War.

Freedom is the cipher that connects the American Revolution, the Civil War, and Watergate. We wrested our freedom from the British, and then our consciousness enlarged, and we extended it to all of our own citizens. This expanded our concept of freedom. Then finally, after another hundred years, we have rescued freedom out of Watergate. This is what our convulsive struggles over the last few years have been about. If the checks and balances of our government had been destroyed, if the two-party system had been wrecked, then freedom would have been gone. Freedom is a terribly difficult concept to understand; unless we protect it for everybody, we cannot secure it for anybody.

It will be a long, long time before we finally realize that we can't take freedom away from our enemies if we want to preserve it for ourselves. We are still playing around with no-knock laws and illegal narcotics raids and talking about being merciless to drug pushers. Okay, but don't expect to have freedom for anybody—maybe more efficient law enforcement, but not freedom.

There were all sorts of economic reasons for the Civil War, but in retrospect the war was fought over moral issues and for the preservation of the nation. The fallout in the American consciousness had to do with moral accomplishment, and it laid a powerful emphasis on human values. Of course, this is not the way the South saw it at the time. Only now is the Southern consciousness beginning to sort out this enormously costly effort for freedom as being the one positive result in the maelstrom of economic, psychic, and cultural destruction that it endured.

The Civil War and Watergate have changed the way we think. The trauma and the disruption are not comparable, but both events were acted out on the field of the American conscience. In a true sense, both gave us a *new* conscience. Of course, a *new politics* will be clearly seen to have emerged from Watergate. We have been stirred up to the depth of our identity as a nation and have come to face new realities as a people. Somehow, crisis has blasted us loose from our massive composure. Our destiny as a nation will be put back into our own hands.

The benefits of Watergate will be manifold. And the further the process goes, the greater the transparency of justice done, the clearer the judgments rendered, the more salutary the ultimate effect of this whole experience will be for the American people. It has been just about the most fateful history lesson that we have ever had. The contemporary political behavior revealed by Watergate has been held up against the unforgiving moral values that are a part of our legacy as a nation. The full implications make even the cynical old pols quake. It is fouling the wellspring. The whole of Watergate under examination gives corruption a bad name.

We don't expect honest politicians, but there has got to be a limit to the thievery. They háve stolen our confidence that our system of government is foolproof. They have stolen our complacency about the checks and balances, and they almost got at the mechanism that makes it possible for our government to right itself when it is tipped.

Unless you understand the reality of a situation, there is no way to do the right thing. But what if there is no moral conscience working, if *right* and *wrong, good* and *evil* have no real meaning for the conscience at hand? We have all seen the specter of that. It has happened to us. It puts the responsibility back on the shoulders of the people where it belongs. When the people realize that they have no one to trust but themselves, they are getting back to the faith that made this whole political experiment possible in the first place. Our form of government is predicated on the principle that all power comes from the people.

According to the polls, a majority of the people think that something is deeply wrong with America. Patrick Caddell, public opinion analyst, says that Watergate has had a significance beyond its own subject, triggering latent doubts and fears created by Vietnam and inflation and other problems. He calls Watergate "an intensifier." According to Caddell's polls, 68 percent of the American people feel that the government has consistently lied to them over the last ten years.[6]

And, yet, according to pollster Louis Harris, "9 in 10 people have not lost faith and are convinced that government can be run well."[7] Putting together the public opinion research in this area, it is obvious that the citizenry has drawn some significant conclusions. We are dealt with cheaply and meanly, and we are run badly, but an overwhelming majority of the people think that our political system is good and sound and that it could be run well.

Our crime is that we have tolerated the sort of politics that has come to afflict us. We have not demanded integrity, honesty, candor, or even love for America. We have pigged it up and allowed our greed to buy our vote, and then we've let the logical consequence of this run wild. Ticking off the persuaders, I come up with chauvinism, law and order, holding the blacks down, leaning on the young, hard line on drugs, and the plain, old, ordinary, garden variety of *greed.* Pure negativism, is what we have been buying.

But why did we buy the *con?* Well, we know that the con always depends on the greed of the sucker. The most outrageous cons work again and again, and it seems miraculous until you understand the power of greed. That little unsavory group of Hessians and worse in the White House worked in an atmosphere that would have repelled bullbats, but it radiated hope for the rich and the reactionary. Most of both would have gone along with anything that would make them richer, punish the poor, and keep the blacks down. They even swallowed the 180° turn on Russia and China. But finally, with the buildup of crises, it got to the point that you had to commit a sort of perceptual suicide not to let any of this get inside of your head. Heads were prised open, and it got in.

So we have all been caught out, not just the crooks. We stumbled around asking each other whether we could still muster moral indignation, and then we were heartened to find that we could. The language of conscience is so uncomfortable to our tongues that it took us forever to call the history emerging from Watergate *immoral, wrong, evil.* And, obviously the conspirators and their fellows had this same problem earlier in the game. As the Jesuits editorialized in their magazine *America:* ". . . one of the chilling revelations has been the complete absence of moral concern at any stage of the conspiracy. The questions asked were pragmatic; the doubts and hesitations concerned expense or deniability. No one asked: Is this just and good?"[8]

In its July 21, 1973, issue, *America* sums up: "Prestige, money, advancement, the usual idols of the 'American dream,' were not completely absent from the motivation of the conspirators. Yet for all that, Watergate still represents a new kind of political corruption. American politics has known before men who abused positions of power for private gain. The Watergate conspiracy betrayed the public trust in more deadly fashion. It stole our birthright."[9]

Having your birthright stolen from right under your nose teaches alertness. Not only had we not been watching it too carefully, but we had also just about forgotten that it was our birthright. Those politicians who were protecting it for us dozed off. But now we've all got new awarenesses, even if our moral vision hasn't entirely come back to us. We can see that we are not going to benefit from losing our freedom. And even the politicians are beginning to get the point of this long, drawn-out morality play. They are tucking in under the tent of the raised consciousness of the people. The pols won't lead, but those who are educable will follow.

The politicans are the ones in trouble. During the last few years they have been disarmed. In fact, "Dick Decent and his decent bunch" have been busy destroying a whole arsenal of political weapons. Partly, this is what the big flap has been about. If you look at it this way, payoffs, kickbacks, squeezes, blackmail, bribery, extortion, influence peddling, perjury, defamation of character, forgery, invasion of privacy, burglary, and systematic subversion of the government agencies, all of these and many more stratagems have been ruined for surviving politicians. The next generation of pols will have to respond to entirely different attitudes of the governed.

This is because we are going to see a pervasive abhorrence

of all of the tacky habits of mind that marked the old regime. The whole wretched electorate has been through a very long course of aversive conditioning. Anybody's behavior could be modified if they were forced to endure endless rounds of sordid revelation that has been our principal political product for so long. There we have been with our eyes propped open and no place to hide. When garbage men become the only officials that the public still trusts, we can surmise that it's because at least they keep taking the offensive stuff away. Nobody is going to vote for more of it.

My own journey through the world of politics has brought me along like a tourist and not a native, but I have learned a few things. I know when man feels imperiled he will vote his prejudices and his low instincts. Any political philosophy that supports what a person conceives to be his own social or economical survival has a powerful appeal. He can hardly be persuaded to reason himself around it. We've got original sin and general orneriness to consider before we can forecast a rebirth of political morality. But despite all of these practical limitations there is a new reality in politics. We are not going to just survive the last few years; we are going to react against them and push off into new perspectives. Look outside and you can see that we are moving.

We have moved out of the landscape of the old politics. It will take us years to process what has happened to our consciousness, but there are all sorts of short-term developments. The post-Watergate morality is a simplistic, immediate response. We have been experiencing all kinds of obvious reform—the equal and opposite reaction to the impact of the conspiracy. All of this is part of the experiential history lesson for the biggest and best taught class in the United States of America. There is no substitute for making the electorate a witness to the secret discourse of politics, give or take a few expletives deleted. This has been pure process and it brought us from back there, up here into different perceptions. The landscape of the new politics is also the locus of a new sort of American conscience about poilitics itself.

The new moral conscience is is working overtime. It is troubled by a lot of things, including our failure to be responsible citizens. There has been a drought of truth in this land. The whole reality of our government's behavior was kept from us. Our politicans neglected us, or lied to us, or both. The watchdogs were all sound asleep. But the false witnesses and the liars have gone so far that there has been a reaction, and the truth might come back into style. We are the witnesses to what has happened to us.

It took a terrible commotion to awaken us, but now we are beginning to exercise the power that is rightfully ours. We will force our values on government. These are the values that we have rediscovered through our national ordeal.

4

BLACKS
Pride and Prejudice

When Martin Luther King, Jr., took over the Montgomery Bus Boycott, it was as if he had suddenly tapped the whole mother lode of black consciousness. I will never forget that February night in 1956 when Dr. King addressed the black community at the First Baptist Church, Negro, at Montgomery, Alabama. I was one of four white people in the church. What was to have been a one-day bus boycott by the blacks had been going on for more than eighty days. A protest over the arrest of seamstress, Rosa Parks, who had refused to move to the back of a city bus, had become a holy crusade. The church that night was filled with a great voice that suddenly found itself and rose out of choked rage and despair. King was speaking, and in effect he said: "We cannot survive in our old lives any longer. You have got to understand what you are doing to us."

The church breathed like a bellows, and the walls seemed to bulge out from the pressure of human emotion. At one point, two men were dissuading a third who was trying to get at me. But then some sort of connection was made, and the hostility against whites turned into a different sort of fervor. The mystical energy and force of the black church was turned loose into the civil rights struggle, and things were never again the same.

That night, chorus after chorus of "We Shall Overcome" came like deafening cannonades. Through some sort of conversion, passive resistance was born, and, spiritually, everybody moved out, singing a hymn of survival.

The new weapon was "love your enemies" and the strategy was to turn the other cheek whatever came and, somehow, to break through to the conscience of mankind. Unknown, at that point, even in the black community, Martin Luther King, Jr., made the connection between the black man's bitter struggle and the white man's conscience, and he became the up-front civil rights leader. But he didn't actually found a movement; he overtook one that had sprung up helter-skelter, sputtering and dying and then coming alive again. All of the disconnected and disorganized sit-ins, wade-ins, and other little bursts of courage and desperation were just waiting to be orchestrated. And, all the while, King was working almost intuitively, putting things together. It was simply a force of soul that he created, something that the black man had not gotten to work for him before.

But the credibility of the Montgomery movement didn't depend on emotional power. It had the smacking reality of another sort of easily understood credential—**solidarity.** That boycott wasn't run by outside agitators or fueled with Communist money or masterminded by European Jews. It was a local, spontaneous movement triggered by a self-respecting black woman who was too tired to move to the back of the bus and give a white person her seat.

The Montgomery Negroes said, "We are not going to pay to be mistreated. We'll walk from now to judgment." As one old man told me, "Our feet are tired, but our souls are rested."

Suddenly, there was this inescapable reality: the black man was being humiliated by the local laws, and he did not like it. He was not going to support this humiliation with his hard-earned money. White emotion ran the gamut from surprise to irritation to dismay to fury to absolute confoundment. The whites were confronted by a stunning unanimity that disarmed all of the rationalizations that they had used to convince themselves and others that *their* black people were happy and contented.

The human face of the black population of Montgomery, about forty thousand, was so evident in that boycott that there was no way it could be denied. The white man had been forced into a position where he had to behave like a human being or behave like an animal or hide. All of us had been hiding from reality in this civil rights struggle for a long time. It took a buildup of crises to crash us through to a radically new awareness that in retrospect seems obvious. At that point in history, a great many things that had been working underground came to the surface and had to be reckoned with.

As a reporter, I had covered the segregation-desegregation struggle of the 1950s from the beginning. And it was in Montgomery that I saw head-on the human face of the black man opposite me. The scales fell from my eyes, and I came face to face with the way the black man had to live—not just out in the streets, but within his own spirit, inside of himself. I couldn't face his lot and say, "Yes, I accept this." Despite my own conditioning and my visceral response, I had to alter my view of him. I could not take the alternative.

Of course it didn't start with Montgomery. During the early '50s, the black man got the white man into some terrible confrontations. It was happening all across the South, visibly and invisibly on all levels of society in both brutal and subtle ways. It had shifted from the test of force that had been going on for two hundred years; now it became a test of soul. In an almost mystical way, a wave of crude conversions began to turn people around. Here and there, the alternatives were laid down: brutalize or do the reasonable thing (not pleasant, but reasonable). Then, increasingly, it was: give up public education or integrate a few Negro children into the white schools—right away. And then people began to make moral reassessments.

Moral reassessments are not spontaneous. They are forced with brute strength and main awkwardness. Consciousness sometimes has to be raised by sheer violence, but then there is an abundance of new perceptions. All the while there is a doomsday background dialogue going on. Everybody says that the quality of life is being destroyed. And in the same breath they say they will die before they let it happen. Actually, people say that they had rather die than sit down next to a black man on a streetcar, or drink at a water fountain with him, or have their kids go to school with his kids, be policed by him, or governed by him—they say this, but they do not mean it. Die-hards do not die hard. It is evident that a great many ritual deaths have to take place before life becomes possible. Why this great negative force?

We'd rather kill people than change our minds about them —a few of us and a few of them. And we have: we've killed blacks trying to get their most basic civil rights in a peaceable way; we've killed kids who threw pine cones at the National Guard; we've killed tens of thousands of women, more deviously, by not letting them have abortions, by shortchanging them with all of the necessities of life (material and immaterial). The greatest sin next to actual murder is killing the spirit; a slick way of going about this is to refuse persistently to let another human being realize his potential. When you find a way to ignore the humanity of the other person, you begin to kill him at that moment. The groups, the individuals, that you want to kill can teach you a great deal about yourself. You can learn a lot about American society by observing who is singled out for punishment. And if you can bring yourself to talk to the people who are punished, you can learn more.

The progress of the Negro through the consciousness of white America has been one of the most interesting odysseys in modern times. The black man has not only produced a durable problem of conscience, the most durable in our social history, he has been a benchmark for comparing levels and inclinations of attitude and their incessant shifts in all regions and in all classes of America. Blacks and our response to them have constituted a dynamic in the growth and evolution of our society. Our cultural and social history would have been radically different and we would be quite a different nation today without them. We would have different distributions of population, wealth, industry, and attitudes.

Blacks collectively serve the United States as a sort of nervous system. They are most exposed to the frictions of economics, the insanity of the homogenizing and the standardizing of man, the dehumanizing of urbanization, and to all of the weaknesses in all of the services of government. They are an early warning system, and they give the alarm, just as the nerve ends in the tips of your fingers give the alarm when you pick up a hot pan. If this didn't happen, sooner or later you would burn your hand off.

They are radioactive and can be located anywhere in the body politic, in the economy, in the cultural and social masses that are generally opaque and almost impenetrable. When they are at the site of an internal disorder, the disorder itself becomes visible. They have, in effect, tagged virulent elements in society and made it possible for us to recognize and observe them. They draw forth the violence and the miscreancy that would be other and less visibly directed. They are the dyes in the bloodstream of the nation, and they signal disease, unhealth, and disorder. They power movements that bend the national consciousness around to perceptions that would be impossible without them.

Rural populations can be ruthlessly exploited almost indefinitely without bringing the "circuit breakers" into action. Workers can be brutalized until jobs literally create physical types. You could recognize a Southern cotton mill worker until

well into this century by his posture, build, and pallor, as well
as by the lint on his head. It took us forever to worry about
women and children working fourteen hours a day, six days a
week. Nobody really worries about the grinding poverty that
perpetually afflicts whole occupations and geographical loca-
tions. If they do, it is spasmodic, and the worry clears up in short
order. Blacks not only have a distinctive color, they attract
exploitation and encourage its investigation. Of course, the process did take a couple of hundred years. Blacks have forced the
investigation of their slavery again and again, and the investigation of one sort of slavery invaribly leads to the investigations
of other sorts of slavery.

This is a fairly brutal role for a people to play out. And this
very fact is recognized and works to the good. The reality of
how these identifiable human beings are treated on all of the
exposed surfaces of life gets into the national consciousness like
an infection in the bloodstream—it holds our attention, it keeps
us from feeling well. Then when it goes critical, it radicalizes
the perception of our citizenry. Anesthetized areas of national
consciousness come awake and feel again. Once the circuitry is
all connected up, the message from reality goes through; and
once you receive it, you can't ignore it.

Help always comes from a distance, and we let the people at
home perish. Easterners could actually feel the pain and hear
the thunk when police clubs hit the defenseless black heads in
Montgomery, Alabama; Southerners all contributed aunts to
the mission field and were fervent in their efforts to save the
heathen Chinese; urban folks worry about California grape
pickers and lettuce pluckers; Methodists worry about the sexual
peccadilloes in Samoa. So it goes with missionary outreach. And
interest is sporadic. Concern with demolished brothers ebbs
and flows more mysteriously than skirts rise and fall, than cuffs
come and go. The black man has come in and out of fashion half
a dozen times since the Civil War. This is true and it is wrong.

The tide doesn't recede as far when it goes out, necessarily, but each time around there is the haunting evidence of unreliability.

Concern for the other fellow's life, liberty, and pursuit of happiness is a delicate and transitory matter. Society's instinct to protect the human spirit is expendable and protean. It may wind up in ecology or in efforts for peace. Contrarywise, an instinct to repress the human spirit could well be expressed in rationales for napalming children. But it can take wild and unexpected forms.

A few years ago, the press reported that a group of fifteen or so Colombian Indians had been frivolously slaughtered for amusement by white ranchers. The defense was that they had always considered Indians as animals, that they had often seen Indian skins sold with other animal skins. They said that it never occurred to them that Indians were human beings. This is a specious defense, but it is also the bottom step on the attitudinal ladder that primitive white people climb at varying rates of speed. If you can get into the frame of mind of the ranchers, you can understand everything about man's inhumanity to man.

Comparatively few Southern Negroes have been killed lightheartedly; about as many as are killed "questionably" by the New York City police. But millions have been demeaned, humiliated, shortchanged in a habit-of-mind sort of way. The black man's sense of identity has been compromised and diminished; his estimate of his own importance has been negotiated down to almost nothing; and the highest art left to him has been an expression of real violence that couldn't be laughed off.

Blacks and children, along with dwarfs, old maids, cripples, albinos, and other orphans of society understand that you can't have a relationship with somebody who refuses to take you seriously. And there is nothing funny about a joking relationship when you are dancing for your supper. Or when you are scrambling for "a let's-pretend" equality to keep your pride together.

As some black man said, "You'll never know the psyhic energy it takes for a black man to just exist." And black men in our society have existed on such precarious terms that if you could really understand the role, you'd have to wonder how any black male could escape with his mental health intact.

It is only a radical potentiality that realizes itself in a hostile atmosphere, and the mind that will not permit change is the most hostile atmosphere. For more than half of this century, the Southern mind was made up about Southern blacks. Negroes were happy the way they were, and they would stay happy if outside troublemakers would stay the hell away from them. "We understand our blacks," or "our Negroes," or "our niggers," well-meaning people of all classes of society said and believed. And the sequitur was, "And they are satisfied with their lives." They could not bring themselves to believe anything else. That sort of mindset has its own field of gravity that holds every black within its reach immobile, captive, with no chance of growing, changing, liberating himself. To break out of the gravity of an imbedded conviction is like breaking away from the gravity of the earth—it takes tremendous force.

Each day of his life, the black man had to cross that mine field —picking his way, trying not to set off anything. He was allowed no self-respecting role. He couldn't be master of his situation, master of his family, or master of himself. There was no way he could protect adequately the welfare of his family. With luck he could protect them from physical intimidation, maybe, but not from psychological assault. And what support he could give depended on where and how he was able to earn a living. Controlling his options was a great power the whites held over him. When you have great difficulty getting credit, you are limited in the sorts of financial security you can ever hope to achieve. The total effect of being psychologically, physically, and financially vulnerable was devastating.

Negroes have been caught in cycles of self-defeat that seem

to regenerate perpetually. Being economically helpless in a materialistic society, blacks never achieve what we call worth. Net worth is the most simplistic and deadly measuring device ever developed. It diminishes everything it measures—big or little. And not having any money means not knowing how to manipulate material things. These can include knives and forks, napkins and finger bowls, tennis rackets, French menus, invitations, Scotch and soda, etc., etc. Finally, if you do not have material things in our society, you become immaterial.

One alternative is being cultivated as an exotic, pretty much like being a whore. You are desired for a thing, which is a simple-minded, cold, and inhuman sort of invitation to dance. As soon as you start being a person, you stop being black (or for kicks) and the collector loses interest. He wasn't trying to collect anything as complicated as a relationship. Complex human exchange is out. This is why liberals are so unsatisfactory to blacks. The relationship that a liberal seeks is an accelerated sort of tokenism. Negroes don't want to be liked because they are black any more than women want to be hired because they have good legs. This means that the second step is dishearteningly complicated.

Incidentally, one of the mistakes that liberals always make is to think they have to enjoy doing the right thing. Blacks know that you almost never enjoy doing the right thing. Chosing the right in life is an extremely expensive procedure, and my thought is that it almost never works best. As my friend Harry Ashmore, champion of civil rights, once said: "Integration is neither wise nor expedient, but it is the will of God." The will of God is quite a terrifying thing, and the average Old Testament Hebrew wanted to think about it as little as possible. You want to do right, not because you benefit, but because your conscience gives you no choice.

To get anybody to do the right thing you have to present them with a right thing and a wrong thing. There can be only one choice, and you have to put the question to them quite directly as to which choice they want to make. Never before had there been a time in American history when this was done with more clarity and force than in the segregation-desegregation struggle in the South during the fifties and early sixties. It raised fifty years worth of consciousness in a decade. It was pure psychodrama, but with a difference. This exercise was not just for the benefit of the actors although the cast was enormous and in terrible need of therapy. It was for the nation.

It just so happened that the civil rights struggle was wired for sight and sound, and the whole nation was a captive audience. As Marshall McLuhan says, with TV, the nervous systems of all men are connected. And it was through this interconnected circuitry of everybody's nerves that the highly charged impulses of reality were transmitted to the nation. It was a reverse electric shock that gave a dividend of ten thousand new brain cells every time it hit. This may not have added to anybody's intelligence, but it hyped up the national awareness. It was a time of spectacle: beatings by the police, fire hosings, raging police dogs climbing on demonstrators, cavalry charges. All of this finally got the message across—"We're not happy!" It got a question across, too: "How can this be justified?"

When the police club hit the head in Selma, Mississippi, that *thunnnnnnnk* reverberated through the head in Buffalo. Most Southerners, who have had a masterly life-talent for not hearing or seeing anything contrary to what they believe, couldn't avoid taking in these scenes and couldn't endure them either. And miracle of miracles, some of the Southern press told the story like it was; and, being uninvolved, so did a good part of the Northern press. The police had been hitting people on the head forever, but not under TV cameras. If you asked a cop later why he hit a black man on the head, he couldn't tell you because if he could, he wouldn't have hit him in the first place.

Without replaying the decade, it is hard to recapture the

public hysteria, the ferocity, the violence of feeling of the '50s in the South. Before the Supreme Court decision in 1954, which put aside the separate but equal doctrine and fired off the segregation-desegregation struggle in the schools, the South had said *never*. Every politician said *never!* The populace would die before they allowed one little black child to enter one white school. If the schools were integrated, the fabric of Southern society would be destroyed. Mobs were ignited by the slightest incident, and the TV cameras captured their rage. Then, inexorably, from the beginning of the decade to the end, the barriers to integration were pulled down from one end of the South to the other. Finally, an accumulation of crises broke through to one central reality: the people were not going to give up the public schools to preserve segregation.

It is true that the white man had turned the public institutions into his own private preserve. He had kept blacks out of his schools, out of his public parks, playgrounds, and swimming pools; he kept them out of his restaurants and his lunch counters. In the old South, he kept them out of his residential neighborhoods. He kept them in the back of his streetcars and buses and on Jim Crow cars on his railroads. No matter how bad the accommodations for the white man were, the accommodations for the black man were worse.

The black man had no decent public existence at all; he could hardly find a drink of water or a bathroom in any public place outside of black neighborhoods. Every demand that this situation be rectified, each step toward a reasonable, dignified existence, cost great effort and routinely exposed him to grave danger. When he moved in on some crummy lunch counter, he risked having his head split by hostile management or a menacing crowd. And each nerve-wracking move was conceived to be symbolic of a takeover by the blacks.

The resistance in the South was led by the most disreputable elements. White trash manned the barricades. As Harry Ash-

more said, "It was Flem Snopes that rallied around the flag and
not Major Sartoris." And it was Harry himself, who won a Pu-
litzer Prize hammering at an opportunistic governor and the
white mob that combined efforts to defeat the orders of the
court in Little Rock, Arkansas. Harry, Ralph McGill, Hodding
Carter, and a small band of brave men kept, resolutely and
unflinchingly, telling the people the truth, what the real choices
were. And these people and men like them reported the violence, the obscenities, the outrages in full detail and laid the
blame for them right where it belonged—on the lying,
backpeddling politicians. Strategically, this is a necessity. The
Southern experience was a lifetime lesson in the anatomy of
political opportunism; and, as a student of this instruction, I
developed Emerson's corollary: *The function of a politician is
to support the baser instincts of the constituency.* A pol never
shirks this responsibility.

Indifference on a highly charged emotional matter is not a
neutral position; it is an extreme position. Indifference at the
top, on the part of the mayor, governor, police chief, whoever
the relevant authority is, means a license for violence at the
bottom. There is a magnification of intensity from level to level
that ultimately converts cold indifference to hot fury; the whole
social system works like one person gradually losing his temper.
And perspective is one thing that restores calm and sanity,
coming down from the top again. It's the head and the hand,
as it were. Reality is not only constantly being reconfigured by
conversation and nonverbal communication in the moment, it
is slowly, slowly changing for people at large as they are forced
to unlearn and relearn the operating principles of life. Historically, this learning process has been very long, and in the individual mind it is very complex.

You've got to develop the conscience before you can feel the
guilt. Comment on the amount of guilt the South felt about
their treatment of blacks has been pretty ridiculous because, in

the main, the construct of conscience required to register this guilt just didn't exist. It has been potentiated all along, and now the conscience is coming into being. There never was any problem being sorry for individual sufferers or being outraged by physical abuse of black individuals. Decent people were programmed and conditioned to be upset by the spectacle of men, women, and children, who were peaceable, being screamed at, spat on, kicked, beaten, stomped, and so on. Even uninvited rudeness was taboo in a consciousness that was unruffled by systematic denial of basic civil rights. It was all right not to let them vote, but wrong to call them nigger. This was part of the reality that was absorbed with sunshine and rain water.

It seems to me that the new person, the child, is driven to learn about external reality by a tremendous internal force. He or she is also intensively instructed in the beginning by the parent, largely for the parent's convenience. All sorts of things are and are treated as life and death matters: don't eat glass, don't put your head in the fire, don't walk in front of cars, don't put your hand in the fan, and so on. At the same time nature is propelling this little individual to register and investigate a bewildering diversity of phenomena. Powered by a supercharged curiosity and directed by parental guidance, this child of nature and of man is learning all sorts of things under high pressure. The unimportant and the wrong information tends to get just as much stress as the important and right information.

Part of this reality that one has to learn about in order to survive may imperil the other fellow's survival. If you learn that Negroes eat in the kitchen; that they come in by the back door (it is a fairly profound thing to force people to go around to the back of a building and enter by an inferior door); that they call you Mr. and you call them John (even when you are a child); that they do the menial work; that they do not get much education and do not have any choice in life; if you learn this as a part of the reality, to a degree you are stuck with it. You are unlikely to be horrified when you continue to see these operating veri- ties. The amount of rationalizing a person will go through to keep his reality intact is unbelievable. And the reality is sort of a piece; you can't pull threads out of it or the whole damn thing will unravel—you know how that is. The way it is is that you have to be hit on the head with new information. You have to be forced to construct a new reality.

Change is only possible when people unlearn and relearn things. This is such an awesome and unlikely process, particu- larly for that part of our society that is stable and indigenous, that when it occurs it is thought of as being a miracle. It is a curious thing that we conceive it to be a miracle when people change their minds. We do not underestimate the bulldog opacity that maintains in the fixed notions of the ordinary mind. If a person has a change of heart or feeling, that is more under- standable. If a person has a reversal of attitude that makes a marriage possible, or reconciles a child, or converts vengeance to mercy, we call it a change of heart, not a change of mind.

Our sins against the blacks are not regional sins; they are universal. But the process of developing a new conscience, of unlearning and relearning, is a Southern experience. That is why it is unremarkable that the South is now going to have more racial harmony and understanding than any other part of the country. Parenthetically, in the North, take New York City as an example, the reality that kids learn is that blacks are dangerous and hostile and are likely to beat the hell out of them or rape them or something. And this walking-around hostility programmed into the whites is of another variety but just as virulent as the old-fashioned Southern attitude. The white Northerner has a visceral contraction when a black man jostles him on the bus, just as a Southerner does. The anatomy of prejudice is pretty interesting.

Sin is conceived to be something you do that is wrong. It is much more likely to be not doing something that may be right.

Not doing right by a black person, by a woman, by a child, is not taking advantage of the last chance of avoiding an accident for them. Ultimately, it is being unable to change your attitude about any individual in any of these classes of people. It is condemning them to life imprisonment in your old attitude. It is really not any more cruel or inhuman than a death sentence.

Prejudice is prepossession or bias, which means a deaf ear for the information from reality or the truth. That is why the truth is so important and why we can be rightfully angry when it is denied us. If you deny another man the truth, he is not able to do right. It is a deadly way of keeping your brother from realizing his potential. If you do not seek the truth, it is a self-inflicted deprivation.

We have got to change our minds about blacks, not only about their inferiority but about their feelings. There can be no argument about this. We have discounted their humanity. Doing right is a positive, seeking sort of thing; you have to undertake concern. It is unbelievable how indifferent we can be, but I do believe that we are moving from unconsciousness to some new awarenesses.

It is the divinity in man that makes it possible for him to change; it is the inexplicable response to the bestowal of grace. Curiously, the Christian way to say a man has changed his mind is to say that he has been reborn—born again. He is new in himself, he is "new in Christ." This possibility of change is a central concern for religion. It is just as important for society. Spiritual renewal is the route away from the doom of dead, petrified positions on anything. It is pure and simple idolatry to venerate and hold above all else a position or an opinion. Whether the position or opinion is judged to be good or bad is of no moment. Immobility is on the side of death.

The South is coming out of its trauma. The region has been confronted and has been put through a rugged experience of reality therapy. And a new reality is beginning to dawn. This is important in human terms, but beyond this, the information we have gained from it could be immediately valuable to all of society. It doesn't matter whether people are remotely equal or not; it doesn't matter what they deserve. It does not matter what spirit the blacks have when they brace us in our institutions. The important thing is the spirit with which we receive them. It is a question of showing real humanity in dealing reverently with the other man's potentiality. Our past failure to do this has become increasingly a problem of conscience in our time. It takes a while for a complex experience like this to work its way through the consciousness of a people. But even now the South is having all sorts of new perceptions about its treatment of the black man. Most Southerners did not know this would happen. We are actually seeing the formation of a new conscience.

I have said that I don't believe that there is any short-term advantage for the white man in integration. Obviously, it may bring relief of conscience to some, but I am talking about practical advantage on the ground. This is a perfect example of the right thing being inconvenient and impractical. But as we are able to come into a more natural association with black people on all levels of society, there *will be* some advantages. I believe there will be a subtle but vital transference. We won't be getting grief from trapped human beings; we will get a unique contribution from a liberated people.

Surprising benefits are going to become apparent when the blacks are able to approach their potential. There will be a tremendous release of psychic energy that they have been wasting just trying to exist. They can restore to us a lot of the magic that we have lost. Sure, some rare intelligence and technological genius will be available, but where we are bleached out is somewhere else entirely. Our emotional and intuitive and instinctual reserves are depleted, and what blacks call soul, we could use a lot of. Urban corporate man has been dry-cleaned, demythologized; we have lost touch with the earth and our own emotions.

American Negroes have been bypassed by the rampaging materialism; many never bought the ideology of the Protestant Work Ethic; killing yourself working and confusing work with religion are two different things. One takes your body, and the other takes your soul. Ironically, there may be some small advantage in having been left out of the American dream.

If we don't get some social wisdom soon, technology is going to be the end of all of us. There is not going to be a massive transfusion from any source, but a great many forces are working toward the sort of understanding we will need for survival. I think that the blacks bring sort of a folk knowledge that could be a balm for our condition. I know there is a lot of paid-up hate and psychic paralysis in the black community; but once we work this out, these beleaguered people, like the ancient Hebrews, may save their captors.

Then there is the question, Who is captive? If you have to maintain a fantastic amount of pressure to keep the other fellow out of the front door, you don't have any real psychic leisure. Standing on the other fellow to be tall is precarious as well as wrong. Pride of race is great, but you don't earn it by keeping the black man snared in prejudice. There is just no way of ripping off his potential, immobilizing him without immobilizing your own conscience. The sort of pride and prejudice that worked at keeping the black man pinned down blocked off reality. You are the prisoner of the man you can't let up.

The messages from reality have been coming through. This truth can set us free, and that will set black people free. At the time, it was inconceivable that we would ever look back on the Southern experience as being a social breakthrough and not an ordeal. Again, it was a creative and useful result from crisis. And the invisible part of it has been the processing of all of this through the consciences of millions of people. This has been a change of mind.

The new American conscience will not allow us to turn away from the human face next to us.

5

WOMEN
Difference and Indifference

I have been thinking about the relationships in my life that have given shape to the way I feel about women. Along with the obvious effects of having a vivid, indomitable mother, other more casual relationships have changed my perception. A girl named Jane came whistling back into my awareness just recently and I think I know why. Jane raised what was at that point a brand new consciousness.

Jane was about my age, and she lived next door in Charlotte, North Carolina, in the neighborhood of forty years ago. I am trying to sort out my indebtedness to her. I see her against a half-remembered background, but she stands out very clearly. She could have been called plain, and she thought of herself that way, but this is not a good description. Just turning into her teens, she had that haunting quality that is made much of in Southern literature. She had such clarity of purpose and unity of mind and body that her only vulnerability was that she was a girl. In that brief protected interlude between childhood and womanhood, Jane was incomparable.

She was the most unforgettable experience I ever had in women's liberation. Graceful, lean, fast, and unerring, Jane could outrun, outplay, outfight anybody anywhere near her size in the community. She was a natural tennis player and took the girls' title the year she learned the game. Jane was a sort of paladin, reserved, but once engaged, deadly. She had a sweet reluctance and great modesty about her role—it was just her fate to have to put things right.

I have run into a few of these people in the course of my life, and everybody gives them a respectful distance. I salute her, and although I have grown to appreciate less serious talents, Jane was a fateful girl to have known. She helped me understand that a woman could be any sort of a person at all. She was unlimited.

Somewhere in the recesses of our past lives are our own perceptions as children and, much later, as young parents. If we can rediscover them, we can get other perspectives on what happens to girls in our society. We are witnesses; we were part of the chemistry that made it happen. Also, as surely as the process took place in our presence, it also took place in our consciousness. First, we were taught the prohibitions in dealing with girls, and then the prohibitions rooted in our own minds. These early, powerful influences helped determine the way I perceive things today.

As I recall, in the private existence of the family, girls had free rein. They got the full sunshine of happy moments and a generous share of the good impulses. They were discouraged from physical violence or retribution and toward modesty; they were groomed and petted and kept cleaner than boys, with more emphasis. In the affections of their families, and inside their own minds and imaginations, they were encouraged to a rich existence. But then something has always happened to girls during that passage to the adult world.

Boys were sort of thrown out into life. Their violent and dramatic response was approved. Sink or swim; better drowned than duffers; if someone hits you, hit him back. They were admired for their fierce glee and, generally, praised for the gusty embrace of forces and events. There was a happy disregard of their bumps and bruises and all sorts of conscious and unconscious pushes toward hardihood. A competitive spirit was nurtured in boys with all sorts of little contests. There was a natural thrust toward a father's engaging with his little boy in a companionable way in all kinds of outside ventures. He went out with daddy into the world.

Little girls are better coordinated than little boys. They are bigger as babies and can outshove and outrun little boys. Traditionally this has been discouraged. And this discouragement becomes the leading edge of a cautionary influence that plays more and more into the lives of growing girls. Boys soon begin to realize that girls are not involved with the most serious goals and objectives of their lives. Girls are obviously not being programmed in the same calculated way; girls are not competing for the same prizes.

There is a continuous, mounting, invisible relegating of girls into less crucial enterprises. There always are some great tomboys who make heroic efforts to swim against the outgoing tide. They recognize instinctively the effort to compromise them as human beings. It is a sad realization. They are mocked for their efforts and encouraged to be less than they might be. And this effort is so fierce and single-minded that it is hard to believe that grown men and women could find a way to justify the way they feel about and behave toward little girls.

Girls are breaking their hearts to play in Little League, on school basketball teams, tennis teams, to run track, to join ROTC, to serve as policewomen on the beat, to join the Coast Guard, to become FBI agents, to wear hard hats, to climb with the high steel workers. The reason is that this is where the action is. Nature is driving them to learn, experiment, try things, find their whole personalities; and society is saying, wait, you can't do this, hold back. Girls have got to burst the private preserves, one by one, just as the blacks did. This is because no quarter is given. Male chauvinist pigs are well trained to "root hog or die" before they give an inch. Half of society must run a strange obstacle course to win the right to be human beings. Perversely, a folk resistance to competition from the female works in the minds of the males. It will be overcome.

If we watch our children, or the young people around us, and take note of how their departures from tradition frighten us, we catch a clue to how stubbornly set in our ways we are and how loath we are to change. Fathers literally drive their teenage daughters out of their homes simply because they are afraid their minds will be turned over. The final break may come, not because the family moral or social standards are being violated, but because the father's rigidities are being threatened. It is easier to dump a daughter than to confront a new idea.

There is no fear like the fear of facing a new reality. The daughter is the mother of woman just as the child is the father of man. If our women force us to give up our old ideas, they have emptied us of our content, and we cannot recognize ourselves or call ourselves by name. And, besides, who of us has not with the utmost care arranged for somebody that we are superior to, that we outrank?

We men have got to demythologize ourselves before we can understand what we have done to women. We didn't spring forth complete from the head of Zeus. From the time we were tiny little boys we were exhorted to be big boys, not to whimper, not to cry, not to be afraid of dogs or thunder or strangers. The air was charged with what was expected of us as boys. From the beginning, there seemed to be no confusion in the minds of our parents about the differences between the masculine and feminine roles. Little girls were just as big and mean as hell, but our parents coached us to treat them in a way that prefigured the ritual roles we would play in later years.

Men don't think their daughters are inferior, just entirely different. They tend to worry, maybe, about whether they are spoiled, but not at all about whether they are brave or determined or stoical or logical or even curious. Fathers do, however, worry about whether their daughters are bright.

Looking back to my years as a father of three young daughters, I recollect halcyon days. Loving, intimate relationships, unstippled by vagrant concerns, gave me no thought about their willingness to compete, to defend themselves, to initiate, to take the lead, in short, to show the signs of dominance. I will say that I was aware of one cloud in the sky, but it was no bigger than a pocket handkerchief. But it began to grow as they began to grow, and I began to try to protect them as vulnerable women. There was a reversal. Their loving hearts that had unstrung me now triggered my early warning system; from my own intuitive and primordial depths came signals of danger.

I realize that our instinct for protecting daughters can run counter to their welfare. We've got to let them go with their loving hearts, so they can make of the outside world a home. If they go to another home, protected by another man in a traditional way, we feel a little better. Marriage has lost some of its inevitability as to when it takes place, but it surely looks desirable to the mothers and fathers of daughters.

There used to be a little dialogue about the substitution of *cherish* for *obey* in the wedding ceremony. The question went: "Hadn't you rather be cherished than obeyed?" And the predictable chauvinist answer was, "Certainly not." A question *about* the ceremony has turned into a question as to *whether there will be* a ceremony. Without our realizing it, the terms have changed. It is no longer a case of the submissive girl giving up a lot of concrete things like her name for a bunch of abstractions, like promises to stand by in sickness. The whole format of marriage has been changed, mostly psychologically, and the aspects that have traditionally been unfavorable to women have been edited.

Explorations of all sorts of marriages—open, communal, multiple, and homosexual—have been going on with high drama but low incidence. When you read about the possible combination in practice, you'd think that marriage counselors would need to be agronomists and dispatchers as well as lawyers and psychologists. What's happened to the old-fashioned idea of a girl and a boy getting married in church? Nothing has happened to it; actually, it's flourishing. More people and a larger percentage of all people are getting married than ever before. A larger number and percentage are almost certainly living together without the benefit of marriage, but many of them eventually marry each other or other people. The institution of marriage is booming.

Sexual love and respect and kindness and constancy are all still bound together. But frequently they exist in forms that don't initially include marriage. Women have had to dynamite the old concepts about marriage to open up enough room so that they could breathe. Getting married immediately after high school or college used to be obligatory, or a person's self-confidence and public image were damaged. A woman became less and less desirable in the eyes of society, and she was forced into either an unnatural or a furtive sort of social existence if she remained single. Of course, the man as a bachelor continued to have great mobility and enjoyed a protected position in society. This has been another punishing aspect of the double standard.

As for marriage itself, it has been organized as a sort of emotional profit center for the woman. The man has a job which is a separate kingdom and his profit center. He disappears into his job as if he had been caught in an undertow and sucked out of sight. He is likely to create a cultic aura around what he does and to behave like a witch doctor about his profession. When his wife comes down to the office, she puts on her hat and gloves and exhibits the same constraint that she would if she were examining African sculpture at the Museum of Modern Art. He lives in two worlds, and she lives in one; and you can see it when he comes home and puts his feet up. There is no mystique there unless his spouse is a gourmet cook. He is at least coequal in her kingdom, and she is nowhere in his.

Actually, our American culture values a woman for what her husband does since she *doesn't do anything* but make life possible for four or five people. If the husband really doesn't do anything either, it is almost impossible for either one of them to be introduced. When the husband is between jobs, it takes an act of courage for the couple to go out in public. The wife's work goes on: she is involved in loving and tending and fostering and nurturing and administrating the family. This might be as important as selling a lot of soap in the Midwest, but not from a marketing point of view. Neither can you base an identity on it. Society sees to it that she is incomplete.

The folkways of our society have always restricted and censored the sensorial intake of the wife. Risk, chance, hazard, and the unexpected are kept to an irreducible minimum in her life; so a seduction process goes on. The wife is seduced to the comfort and security of close horizons, to unvaried order, to lowered consciousness, to a minimum contact with strangers. If a child is sick or a guest fails to show at a dinner party, she deals with the unforeseen. The inevitable includes the exhausting possibility of having several young children at the same time, but this offers sacrificial and not creative opportunities. She is cast this way, and so this is the husband's image of her, a confined person with the boundaries of her experience tucked in closely and comfortably about her.

All the while, her husband is laying down an indelible stereotype in his mind about his wife, all other wives, and all other women. His early conditioning is being reinforced. He continues to perceive his wife in the usual ways, and her behavior confirms his observations. The force of gravity in her life makes her seem more simple than she is. And she prepares a perfect foil for the liberated or career woman that the husband runs into downtown. When he is crossed by a lively, uninhibited woman who is a complete person, the confrontation sets off warning signals from one end of his ganglia to the other. He only partly perceives her; there's too much reality. He tunes her out and, unless forced to the wall, chooses to believe that she has the lowest possible job and the least possible importance. And he treats her this way.

The career woman is almost inured to the put-down routine; it is an integral part of her every day. She is fatalistic about chauvinism, and she had better be or she can't go out of doors. Sometimes she is saddened or irritated by the hostility that she generates by just existing, but, after all, she has had some early training too. She didn't run the combine, or move stones, or study advanced math, or make the team. She realizes that, apart from genetics, she has gotten her picture of herself from the way those around her have seen her. She has been through the processes of expectation and prohibition. Her parents expected this and demanded that and forbade this. It's all recorded, but she has broken free, and she is a transitional person.

The whole intricate encouragement to make a living, with all of the early-rising admonitions that prefigure the get-a-job push, is a drill that affluent parents do not lay on their daughters. If the girl is expected to earn her living, the expectations rarely go beyond secretarial school or a little graduate work in the library sciences. It affects you not to be expected to do things. The lack of demand is not an intentional slight, but it changes the whole dynamics of the charge to the younger generation. We keep gearing the boys up while we are gearing the girls down.

If you ask a man what he expects of the world for his daughter, you catch him off guard. He may say that he hopes she will marry well and happily, and you know you have a traditionalist on your hands. Most probably he will say that he hopes she gets exactly what she wants out of life, whatever it is that will make her happy. He means this, but it is still difficult for him to imagine her in a business situation that involves her directing a group of men. Of course the daughter finds it difficult too because her experience has been with a very private sort of power.

Our dilemma of mind is that we are caught between two feelings—we want our daughters to change, and we want them to stay just the way they are. We can't bear for our own girls to lose any of their tenderness or delicacy of spirit because this is the way we remember them, this is the engram in our minds. And in our own psyches, it is unchangeable. It is useful to talk about *our* daughters since this is the surest pathway to the masculine conscience. Other men's daughters get to be more of a problem.

A very successful and intelligent businessman was talking to me about his daughter. "My girl is in banking," he said. "She is so smart that if she were a boy, I'd take her into my business as a partner." Why not? Take her in, I thought, and call it Parkens & Daughter. It would make a great hit. Beside the impact, you couldn't imagine what a female intelligence would do for that firm. Men always think that women are dumber than they are, and that is the only advantage that anybody ever needs in business. There is a good chance that woman is as complementary to man in work as she is in play. This has been my experience.

You'd have to be a transvestite in drag to report on the putdowns that successful career women experience in the business world. Say that our composite businesswoman is young, attractive, carefully dressed, and cheerful looking—the attributes that are winning in most situations. She doesn't have the glazed look of the business-bent executive or his funeral-parlor pallor. In this instance, she is outward bound. She is moving against traffic at any of the terminals where the commuters come in the morning and go out at night. All the men notice her, and they make up 90 percent of the travelers. Obviously, she is a secretary going in the wrong direction. She is going away from work. "Where you going?" "You're going to be late." "Don't you know your office is that way?" And so it goes.

Our lady executive completes this trip and finally gets back to her office. There is an accountant in the waiting room; he has answered an ad in the morning paper and has come for an interview. She speaks to him pleasantly. He ignores her. He is amazed to find, twenty minutes later, that she is one of the principals across the table from him, interviewing him. Anybody who sees this young lady in the office without getting any clues, that is, when she is not in her own office or with her secretary, probably speaks of her as "the girl"—this is the style. And he may do this with a tone that suggests that she is an object and not a person. "Lèt the girl do this," he'll say.

This lady executive is an inside board member, and there is a board meeting that morning. She is asked to take the minutes (an assumption of secretarial competence and responsiveness to male directive), and since the meeting includes lunch, she is expected to serve the sandwiches or preside over the service. This might be all right if the communicative impulse suggested hostess rather than waitress. As the meeting gets underway, the men function as a club, and far from performing as individuals at this board meeting, they will reveal all sorts of subtle indications of interlocking assumptions, interests, prior agreements, and subserviences. If she raises a sticky question, they will work together to finesse it. They will mount a force of countervailing opinion; they will smother her.

Now this is interesting. If a woman forces the issue, she is becoming emotional, and that is counterproductive and unprofessional. If a male forces an issue, he is showing dominance and asserting leadership that is becoming to an officer of a corporation. It creates a strained air of embarrassment when a woman forces her point. But I have seen a board keep its composure when one man threatened to castrate another.

Our lady, who happens also to be a founder of this business, goes to the bank, and although her signature is on file, she will be seen as a secretary by male and female employees and bank guard alike. To withdraw a thousand dollars from her own savings account, she has to negotiate. Some minor officer will give his written okay. All awaɪe of the transaction will assume that the money is either for a vacation or an abortion.

Back at the office Ms. Executive will have her signature on any note that pledges personal collateral, but she will notice that she is not always invited to meetings with the underwriter or the lawyers. Of course, if the underwriting falls through, and the loan is called, she will be taken for everything the bank can get their hands on. In the quieter moments between calamities, when the day's work goes into the evening or if she is in another city doing business for the company, she will enjoy all of the considerations given an escapee from a mental institution who is still wearing the hospital uniform. In short, the problems of eating and drinking, casually, elegantly, alone, can be pestiferous.

If there is a late meeting down in Wall Street at The Bankers Club of America, she will find that they do not serve ladies in the bar and that there is no ladies room. She will have to use the servants bathroom. This in the face of the fact that women control most of the money that they are doing business with down at the banks. My thought is that women united should use a substantial portion of this money for a spirited and terrible revenge.

When cheerful, hopeful people, anxious to do the right thing have to go through all of this grief, something is wrong. If it is just because of a couple of chromosomes, it makes you wonder. It makes you wonder about the character of the opposing chromosomes.

Pass over the fact that you need the charisma of Joan of Arc and the guile of Lucrezia Borgia to wring a vice-presidency out of a respectable corporation if you are a woman. After you get it, you still live with male chauvinism. But then, with this sort of talent, you can put up with put-downs.

"Years after I became partners with my former boss," a successful lady executive says, "all men still refer to him as my boss. When you are with a man, it is always assumed that *he* is *your* boss. Men do not want to and will not think otherwise." She is philosophical about this, but it is still discouraging for her.

Considering that we are living in a democratic society, the successful white American businessman may be the champion male chauvinist. He may also be one of the most vulnerable members of contemporary society, vulnerable to change—the best-adjusted always are. His women are changing, and his children are changing, not radically, maybe, but they are definitely in touch with a new reality. There is a whole pattern of possibility for him in terms of what is happening to the women around him. As his consciousness is raised about women, he will begin to make certain discoveries. For the first time in our society the essential femaleness of man will begin to express itself.

Nobody is 100 percent male or 100 percent female, and a good thing. Men are part feminine, and women are part masculine; liberation for women will inevitably liberate the other parts of both sexes. Men who want to tend babies, grow flowers, cook, clean, sew, put up strawberry jam—these cats will breathe easy and send their wives out to work. It would be marvelous if this sexual role casting that we indulge in could be relaxed and if people could be their whole selves. This would be a true blow struck for diversity. If the kinky could unkink a little bit in their daily lives by doing their thing, a tremendous amount of good energy could be released for all manner of worthwhile endeavors.

The idea that women are not necessarily inferior is beginning to penetrate the collective, self-protected male consciousness.

The message is even reaching women. Some have heard the rumor before and have passed it along; for the first time they are internalizing it. The happy, unreflective male chauvinism of the past is on the way out. It will remain a designation like being a Democrat or a Republican, but it won't be a major party. The old tapes will play on and on, but at least there is some chance of critical feedback.

One sad thing is that women will never make it until they overcome their natural need to be adored, to be "respected." Certainly the women's lib group has made a start; they have disparaged marriage, flouted convention, and have gotten everybody's attention. The major accomplishment is that a great many women have made it absolutely clear that they are not happy. This is the momentous message, and it registers. If women are not happy, then all of us have done something wrong, and this becomes a problem of conscience.

The new American conscience is processing all sorts of questions about the way we have treated women, the way we have prevented them from reaching their potentials. The new awareness between the sexes portends one of the most profound awakenings that we could possibly experience. Men are beginning to realize the implications of the revolutionary new choice women have on conception. Gratification and reproduction have been finally separated despite man's heroic effort to keep them indissolubly bound. Now, if a woman takes the pill, it is not possible to nail her with childbirth, consciously or unconsciously. The heated considerations of the population explosion have had a good side effect. You now can do a version of the right thing by not having children as surely as you can by having them. It is nobody's business but one's own—ultimately, the woman's.

All of the hostility that men have expressed by knocking up women will have to be expressed in some other way—possibly without the blessing of society.

Man is bewildered and distraught because woman is turning and walking away from him into new experiences. Woman is in the process of being reborn. Man is never so helpless as when woman walks away; he cannot deal with this. If women could understand this simple strategy, they could win any quarrel by walking away from it. Obviously, this technique is limited in terms of solving problems, but it surely resolves situations.

Men and women use such a small part of their mental potential that it doesn't make the slightest bit of difference if either sex is theoretically more intelligent than the other. The point is that women are acculturated to stylized and limited roles. This defeats the good sense and instinct that nature gave them in the first place. Research indicates that when you feed a wild turkey, it takes nine generations for the line to recover the powers that a turkey has in its untampered-with state. It should not take a human being as long as a turkey, but the American woman will continue to evolve through a succession of rebirths.

As a class, women have been excluded from everything. Blacks have had the same experience as a race, and the parallels are riveting. Like blacks, women have had to overturn existing law and then overcome the cunning and malice of their adversaries. We didn't learn anything from the racial wars. Emblematically, the black has had to become white, and the woman is having to become man in order to pass the sentinels of the male preserve where all of the rewards are kept. "Advance, friend, and be recognized."

Friend is an interesting concept in the male-female relationship. In the past, only very liberated men and homosexuals have been friends with women in our society. If you are a man, friendship with a woman is a tricky business, and on the face of it, unacceptable to most people. There are taboos against this sort of thing, and it is certain to be misunderstood. In polite groups it sometimes seems that only gay men have real ongoing relationships with women as people. Though it seems inexplicable when women knowingly marry homosexuals, there is a congeniality there that women despair of finding with heterosexual men.

It is ironic that men have to break out of the magnetic field of straight masculinity to avail themselves of an adult relationship with half of the members of the human race. I think that marriage is the only front that offers enough concealment for true friendship between the sexes. Even married men have to be careful in describing their relationships with their wives. Our culture doesn't prepare us to accept the fact that a man can have a rich, deep friendship with a woman. Of course this has been changing. The younger generation has already worked it out in a preliminary sort of way, and they will have a brand-new benefit if they don't relapse.

The young are growing up with a great equality between the sexes. Sometimes the lines actually seem blurred to us. They wear the same clothes, have hair the same length, affect the same life-styles, and take the same sort of risks in life. They also take better care of each other and they have a much more loving society. They seem to be less suspicious of each other and less afraid of life. They do not have the same violence inside of themselves, and they do not seem to invite it to the same degree from the outside. Since boys and girls are friends, they mutually enjoy a richer intake of social experience and have more complex relationships. They tend to think of each other as individuals, and not just as sexual objects. On the surface, this is a significant social phenomenon, as yet unmeasured as to extent, but real. There is no way to calculate the ultimate effect this will have on girls. It could revolutionize the way this generation of women see themselves.

The prisons have not been torn down yet, but the new regime is releasing prisoners by the millions. The homely and plain are not left out of life forever, bound to house arrest by the neglect of men. They are backpacking in Afghanistan where they don't

look so homely and plain. And besides, the century of the con-
fection is over. Styles and ideals have changed. The new-style
female dresses down and grooms down to such a degree that life
is no longer a beauty contest. Other values are becoming visible
and are registering. The fate of the wallflower is in transition;
the old-maid label has been dissolved. The freemasonry of the
younger generation is changing the life-style and the perception of the girls of today. The old security has been assailed by
new risks, but the doors to life have been thrown open, and the
options are popping up like spring flowers.

It is interesting that the allies of the younger generation have
been the women of our society and not the men. Mothers have
stayed in touch with their long-haired boys, and, spiritually,
many of them have understood the passions of the younger
generation. Mothers have marched for peace and have stood for
amnesty, and they have been the agents of reconciliation in the
generational struggle. It has been a decade of remarkable
change within the awareness of the average middle-class
woman.

All women are obviously not alike, and nothing has been
done in concert. But female responsiveness to human rights has
been increasingly conspicuous—almost massive. It has been
inevitable that in striving for more satisfying and expressive
lives for themselves, they would have all sorts of new perceptions. Their consciousnesses have been raised. Women have
communicated this to each other in a positively electric way,
and the new faith of having more faith in themselves has been
highly contagious.

One concept that women have always understood intuitively
and are now proclaiming is that *being* is as important as *doing.*
The very lives of most women have been pure research in this
area. When your work is classified as *homemaking* and your
identity is *housewife,* you have to specialize in *being.* A woman
may think of herself as being somebody's wife, but she does not

have her identity entangled with Continental Can or Union Carbide. She doesn't introduce herself by saying what she sells or feel more or less worthy if sales rise or fall. To a degree, women operate out of themselves as individuals. This means they are in better touch with their own emotions and are closer to reality.

Our exploitation of women has involved a long process of denying them the right to be what they are and conditioning them to be what they could not naturally become. Romanticism is a cop-out. It's a circuit breaker that keeps the voltage between the sexes from becoming unmanageable. When we talk about the difference between man and woman, we are gilding a masculine dream. We are playing with ourselves and toying with women. *Vive la différence* is finally translated as indifference. Human nature works against equity for the "associate" members of life.

If women are as different from us as we think, then we need them more. If not, what is our problem? It is more than possible that a renaissance is bottled up in the available feminine intelligence, wit, intuition, and warmth and in the clarity with which women perceive reality. They could help us as a people gain momentum in the right direction for survival.

Self-discovery is almost always awkward and unattractive from the outside. Inside it is likely to be pandemonium. Aside from presentation and style, becoming separate and complete involves a profound reordering of one's self. Past this crisis there are unbelievable opportunities for growth and change. This is the business that women are about today—moving toward a very different future at varying rates of speed and with varying degrees of grace. This is happening across society to all classes and conditions. As dramatic as the fanfare is, the invisible changes within the consciousness of women and of men are much more fateful.

In retrospect we will not be able to understand why we have

treated women the way we have or why they have tolerated it for so long. It took this much violence to break through to the reality of how we feel and behave. This awareness has shattered the old chauvinistic composure, and it cannot be put back together. The new American conscience is at work, and it will deal with the relationships between the sexes on entirely different terms from now on.

Again, we are on a divide, and the land that falls away in front of us leads into a new wilderness territory. The experience of man and woman together will be epic. But then, so will everything else.

SEX

Innocence and Guilt

I can hear the warm, concerned voice of a college professor out of the past. It was a spring day, and the air was haunted with the murmurings of the earth coming alive. In that small Southern town any moment in time had a natural connection to the past; so I was able to accept the solemn echo from the nineteenth century as a friendly anachronism. "Gentlemen," my teacher said, "I hope you will forgive a very personal comment. After we were married, I had intercourse with my wife once, and we had a child. Some time after that, we had intercourse a second time, and there was no child. I accepted this as a sign from God that we were to have no more sexual relations."

This was not some embarrassing confession or neurotic exhibitionism of any sort; it was a "moral insight" meant for instruction and born out of the experience of a devout biblical scholar who felt that training the young was a sacred trust. It was iconic, even in 1941. This was *straight arrow, circa 1880,* a dying resonance of the Victorian era. To my mind, the striking thing is that there was at that time a tenuous credibility to this sort of witness.

What an extraordinary experience it is for me to be able to bring the tolling of that clear bell back into my mind. For the

God-fearing, prudent, ascetic man or woman, there was the sort of purified existence that is incomprehensible now. To us then, this moralizing sounded incredibly innocent, but not insane, not perverse. I mean, this attitude could live in the garden of ideas that was part of our scenery—at the edge of the garden, but within the pale. There was then, although certainly in its last days, a Garden of Eden view of sex, the vestigial remain of an old covenant not to eat all of the fruit. It was an enchanted sort of innocence that had nothing much to do with life before or life after.

The sexual revolution is mind-boggling, but not in terms of what people are doing. An underground of this has been around us from the beginning of time. I am stunned by what has happened inside of people's minds—all people, everywhere, of all ages. When people begin to consent to radically different moral values for themselves, their children, and others, the psychic displacements are profound. There is a whole new internal scenario for behavior in one of the most tumultuous, ungovernable, unpredictable areas of life. Given a description of contemporary sexual behavior, what would Freud have deduced about the society?

College coeds talk wistfully about the good old days ten years ago when students just dated. I suppose there are still secret daters all over the place, clandestine virgins, dropouts from the revolution. You can get hurt in this hand-to-hand combat, but nobody loves conscientious objectors—they make the troops look silly. Kenneth and Betty Woodward talked to students and college officials all over the country in researching a report on casual sex, and they discovered tremendous peer-group pressure on students to liberate themselves sexually. No single male student would admit to them that he was a virgin. "You could get more people to admit they are homosexuals," one student said. And Dr. Richard V. Lee, of the Yale School of Medicine, told them: "To my mind, this new sexual ideology is as dictatorial and cruel as Victorian prudery."[1]

This isn't a slow-breaking change in sexual attitudes or behavior; it is a quick reversal. In less than ten years, the virgin and the nonvirgin have changed roles. In a curious turnabout, girls now have to mount an awesome psychological defense to retain and defend their virginity. A sustained physical effort is likely to be required too. The revelation of the young is that sex isn't a solution; it's a problem. Not having it is a problem; having it is a problem. Having sex demanded is one thing. Having it expected more casually than the old goodnight kiss is a new game. Not by any means is everybody playing that game, but everybody can hear the band strike up down at the stadium, and back in their rooms, maybe a little lonely, they know the game is going on.

Since man thinks about sex every few seconds, it is reasonable to believe that having it or not having it could make quite a big difference in his state of mind. But what sort of difference? Not long ago, I went back to that marvelous college where we had all lived comparatively continent lives, and delivered a speech. I could look across from the speakers stand, under the great elms and oaks, and see the window of the classroom where more than thirty years before I had been gently instructed in God's attitude about fornication. I thought about the earlier pronouncement, but I didn't grasp the new reality until that night.

After the entertainment, we were walking back through the luminous twilight up past the familiar row of dorms, and then I got the news. It was like a case of *déjà vu:* windows were lighted; students were in the same, eternal attitudes on the steps. An imperishable sensation of time past began coming unlocked in my mind—then the new society. Light, sort of giggly female laughter came out of the dorm windows, here and there like spots of bright sound. In that moment, that place was a sturdy grid against which I could measure change.

I had to admit that the change meant that a whole cast of mind was gone, in the graveyard. When I had been a student there, the trustees of the college forbade us to dance within the town limits. This ban against ballroom dancing, touch dancing, as they call it now, was an anomaly and not characteristic of the atmosphere of that decade. But the fact of it gave me a very precise starting point for measuring the trip that I had taken in the intervening years. Half humorously, I wondered what the girls and boys were doing up in those rooms—dancing?

Revolutions are always based on old realities as well as on new demands. Obviously, the old time is exhausted and pure tinder before it can be lit and incinerated. I am sure that all revolutions are old news to those who are aware of what is happening, that all successful ones are long overdue. It's life's most common experience that people, corporations, institutions, governments live long after there is any possible explanation for it. The old sexual morality, the old sense of sin—how comfortable were they on us when we had them, and how could they wear out that way, without our being aware of it? It seems our children might have told us what was going on.

The generations are tied together like mountain climbers, traversing some sheer face of rock. The last generation is climbing; the middle generation is picking at the crevices; and the oldest generation is hanging on and thinking about earlier climbs. Like mountains, complex, evolving relationships cannot be completely understood from one point of view or one point in time. One of the most fascinating perspectives to climb over is the generational curve in attitudes about sex and marriage.

My mother told me about a friend's daughter who had run away to Mexico City with a disreputable character. He was an overage hippie whose only visible talent was seducing young girls.

"I certainly hope she married him," my mother said.

"I certainly hope she didn't," I said.

"Why would she have bothered?" my daughter asked.

Which is most damaging, and to whom, a disastrous marriage or an unsavory premarital sexual experience? If you take a billy goat to bed, is it better to do it under sacred covenant of marriage? The old concept of the ruined life is not very popular anymore. And for women this is liberation in the true sense. At least there is some special dispensation whereby today's families are able to blink at happenings that would have forced an old-fashioned family to move out of town, or the head of the family to commit premeditated murder. This is a revolutionary difference.

The new American conscience had come through a profound metamorphosis. As our consciousness has been raised in the last generation, an abundance of new perceptions about sexuality have brought us into impact with new realities. We have for the first time in about five hundred years become aware that women enjoy sex just as much as, if not more than, men. The hostage half of the human race has been freed from bondage by contraception; this sexual emancipation of women will release incalculable energy into our society. This liberation movement will pour down serendipitous benefits. New codes of behavior and accountability will be worked out on the personal level, and although this will be painful and will produce many casualties, sexually we are coming into a new Augustinian age.

When I was a boy, premarital sex was rated along with cannibalism, bestiality, and infanticide. The one admonition about sex was **don't**. The taboo had great energy, and it was directed at the flammable chemicals of growth in the life of the adolescent boy and girl. Anguish, torment, conflict—all leading to excruciating ambivalence and settling out in the form of guilt was the inheritance of the post-Victorian progeny of the repressed ages. The only way of assessing the psychological damage done to the victims of *Sex is dirty* and *Don't* is to look at the contrasting attitudes of the younger generation.

Sex itself had to break out of the closet before the specialties could escape. Obviously there have been a lot of escapes, really miraculous escapes, by individuals, but the whole generation that is now fifty has either dropped out of real life or been reeducated about sex. It is preposterous that before the turn of the century, books by male and female authors were not put next to each other in the library, but it is more remarkable that real live human beings were treated this arbitrarily. Regional, rooted, conservative, and devout families across the nation created fear of the opposite sex that turned men and women into hostile strangers. In those good old days there was no question about what was right and what was wrong.

It was perfectly clear what was right and wrong in sex; right was not doing it. You could be sure you were good if you didn't do it. A virtuous woman didn't have to be a good, kind, considerate, hospitable, truthful, honorable person. She was virtuous if she didn't do it. Women stood next to their little boys in church while the pastor read from the Old Ṭestament: "In sin did my mother conceive me." They repeated this libel and did not raise a complaint. So when a young woman was in the protective covenant of matrimony, and she had the permission of society to *do it*, it was still wrong and sinful in the eyes of the church. Society had further helpful comments for women who were grudgingly allowed to do it: "This is your burden. You will have to bear it for the sake of the *beast*, not the divine spark but the beast in your husband. And you will not enjoy it."

Is there any wonder that most orgasmic women were fairly quiet about it since even their own partners were not educated to appreciate this possibility. Sex was hardly a celebrative experience in America during the early part of this century. There wasn't any easy-going approach to these rites of passage, either; sexual awakening was baffled by near hysterical prohibitions concerning nudity and masturbation (called self-abuse), and there was a total lack of useful information. Boys were told certain things, however, such as: masturbation would drive you insane, make *it* fall off, make hair grow in your palm, and that generally it was wicked and evil to play with yourself. Everybody did, of course, but they felt wicked and evil and were tormented by anguished consciences that were never given any rest. My most familiar recollection of childhood is that of being continually stricken with guilt.

I am sure that girls were not given as many explicit directions except in the area of keeping their skirts down, their backs turned, and their pants up. But the whole atmosphere around pubescent girls was loaded with dire warnings of what would happen if unspeakable things were done, shown, or even thought about. When these girls finally became women and somebody had to tell them what was happening to them, not that they had not already discussed this with each other, it was done with cold impersonality. Parents shoved books into the hands of little girls, hopefully in time to keep them from thinking they were bleeding to death.

This whole business worked out very well in its own negative terms. A vast majority of women were virgins when they married. Since nice girls didn't do it, with the help of constant vigilance from mother, father, and conscience, they didn't do it—but the concentration on *it* did give them a mechanistic, self-conscious, inhuman attitude about sex. The *it* became a sex object that they, with the aid of sobriety, dexterity, and panty girdles, were protecting from every man who was after that one thing that he had to have to pass the puberty rite and prove he was a man.

Of course, this little highly marketable goody was bartered for marriage. The father who owned his daughter in our materialistic society, boxed her and *it* until he turned her over to a suitable young man who would keep her in a box until she had good little babies. Then the girl babies would be kept in a box until they were turned over to another generation of young men.

As long as you own a woman, her value is enormously enhanced by her virginity. When she owns herself as most girls do these days, she may wonder why virginity is such a big thing. As she begins to think of herself as something more than an associate member of the human race, it begins to seem degrading that her whole value is calculated on the basis of whether she is intact or not. What sort of an accomplishment is that? How can a person's desirability be determined by such an irrelevant, negative, and downright embarrassing physical detail?

For the younger generation, sex has become another area in life in which a person can behave well or badly. The ordinary virtues that apply to all of the rest of life can be applied here. Keeping your word; being honest and truthful; being kind and charitable and showing concern for others—all are applicable to a person's sex life. In the new consciousness, girls have realized that they have to ask themselves: "Am I being true to myself?" "Am I hurting somebody?" "Is there enough love and affection to support my response?" This could be part of a positive approach to loving. After all, *not doing it* didn't really seem to have any relationship to anything. When you made not doing it a virtue, it became a rigid thing like the worship of law. This is almost idolatry. And it thwarts the life force. The new conscience will work within these awarenesses.

The role of conscience under the rules of the old code was pretty clear-cut. But all of this gave sex a very heavy quality; and it put a lot of strain on the ultimate resolution of relationships. There was no laughter, no humor in sexual love American style. And the admonitions and the prohibitions were the unfunniest of all. While boys and girls in the rural South were being told that the reward for fornication was hell fire, nice little Catholic girls in New York City were being told by their nuns that it was a sin to wear lipstick and a sin to wear highly polished patent leather shoes because boys could look into them and see their pants.

We were being conditioned out of all of our natural responses to the opposite sex. In the more puritanical circles, the sexual legacy was being spoiled for all time. Men were being denied their great potential capacity for loving women, for ultimately living with them in the light and warmth of full sensuality. Consciousness was being constricted, lowered; and reality was being obscured by puritanical design. The perceptions of that time and climate were limited to the old perspectives that had been salvaged and resurrected, but powerful forces in our society had already doomed this holding action.

The twentieth century was not the nineteenth century. Before World War II we were moving to the second great divide in human history. The imprinting that had gone on long before would control the lives of the older generations; they might remain hostages to an old conscience. Change would speed up from rapid to drastic. Soon the new perceptions would inform the new conscience. The sexual revolution is not in any sense a carnival of aberrational lascivious behavior; it is a profound evolution of new relationships between men and women.

It is almost impossible to get the mind around the basic concepts of the old morality. It ignored the fact that almost all of life is relationships. In every relationship you are responsible for the people you deal with. You are responsible for the people that you party with, the people you play tennis with and sail with and drink cocktails with. You are responsible for the people that you rescue the poor with, provide the life and sustenance of art museums with, and instruct people how not to have babies with. You are also responsible for the people that you sleep with. What a weird idea.

As for the new morality, it includes a heightened and broadened appreciation of sex and more sexual activity of the heterosexual variety for the married and unmarried in every age group. But a great part of this takes place within the context of love, devotion, and a monogamous intent, inside or outside of marriage.

Doubtless there has been a lot of conversion from youth up, but age itself is the dominant variable in determining how people will behave sexually. The new American conscience is available to all ages, and there is a substantial increase in frequency and variety of sex at all age levels. But the fruits of the sexual revolution belong to the young, and they are living a more spontaneous and less guilt-ridden life without jeopardizing the basic concepts of marriage or embracing purely recreational sex. On the basis of a comprehensive survey[2] of the sexual behavior and attitudes of the American people, *Playboy* magazine has been able to draw some firm conclusions.

Playboy may be a little disconcerted that swinging is a very minor theme in the new morality, but they manfully admit in summary: ". . . many contemporary Americans are somewhat less fettered in enjoying their sensations than their precursors were; but by and large, they have added to their regular repertoires only acts that are biologically and psychologically free from pathology, they have remained highly discriminating in their choice of sexual partners and they continue to attach deep emotional significance to their sexual acts rather than regarding them as sources of uncomplicated sensuous gratification."[3]

The *Playboy* study was carefully cast to explore the principal areas investigated twenty-five years ago by Alfred Kinsey in his landmark study of American sexuality. This makes it possible to measure changes in attitudes and behavior over the last twenty-five years. The inhibitions that Kinsey discovered during the '40s have been replaced largely by what *Playboy* calls "permissiveness with affection." For instance, contemporary premarital sex is described as "a loving relationship [that] still has marriage as its implied goal—and the quality of sex within marriage still seems to be integrally connected to the strength and security of the emotional relationship."[4]

The whole population used to break around major variables, with educational level, degree of devoutness, political persuasion, social class, and economic position determining sexual attitudes and behavior more profoundly than age. This is no longer true. The young have overcome all sorts of other differences to agree about sexual behavior—young white- and blue-collar workers are closer than father and son, at least theoretically. That means we have a generational swing out of the old Victorian orbit into a much more congenial atmosphere. However, the new role requires the exercise of a great deal of responsibility for decision making—not just whether, but with whom, how, and under what circumstances. This means that we are coming into much more sophisticated problems of conscience.

The cold-blooded bargaining of technical virginity for security, that is, marriage, is out of style. When girls were a *thing* and what they had to give or withold was a thing, they were purchased through a sort of ritual transaction known as courtship. Everybody's mind was so absorbed with the mating game that identities got lost along the way, and, typically, newly married couples found each other to be hostile strangers. They had married as a conclusion to a highly stylized sort of hide-and-seek that might have been going on for three months or three years.

The rules of the game were terribly complex and codified, and since instinct was no guide, instruction books were sold by whoever wrote the advice-to-the–lovelorn column in the daily paper. A title for this how-not-to booklet might be *Rules for Necking and Petting* and it always spelled out a game plan that told a young lady of say, fifteen, what she could and couldn't do on the first, second, third, and on to infinity dates. There never was any really satisfactory way to deprogram this same girl five years and twenty cycles later or whenever marriage took place. After stalling all of her systems for years, could she fire them up again?

The old procedure was useful since it kept the girls from thinking or feeling and removed responsibility from the shoulders of the boy. He just never had to deal with anything as complicated as ardor or affection, and he certainly never had to figure out anything for himself or make an original move. The really harmful and costly effect was that both sexes were conditioned to accept the values of the system. The loving natures of two human beings in this sort of relationship were likely to be thwarted and repressed until they weren't loving anymore. And boys believed that nice girls didn't do it; so any high-spirited, sensuous girl who enthusiastically did do it would be used and rejected. The unloving could play this game safely, but the loving were trapped.

This was a double standard, self-reinforcing, and it had many implications. The boys were expected to do some prowling, playing the field, and it was assumed that they would get all of the sexual experience that they could roust up and were ready for. This did not make them less desirable in the eyes of the girls or of society. Since girls were not supposed to have any sex until they were married, the girls these boys lucked up on were likely to be damaged in reputation and self-esteem. The girls couldn't initiate anything; they could not call boys on the telephone or go to see them. They could wait. This was the era of the wall-flower, and some girls waited forever. Some are still waiting thirty years later. The overlooked girls might not seem at all undesirable according to objective standards. Some were too striking looking, and they frightened the boys; some were too smart; but the majority were saddled with the usual obstacles to popularity. It was a cruel time, and it is well behind us.

The breakdown of the double standard is one of the most interesting developments in the sexual revolution. The girls of today have swapped inhibitions, social pressure, and some neuroses (and a lot of boredom) for an array of problems of conscience. Obviously, it was always possible to be conscience-stricken over minor infractions of the code, over the legalistic considerations that came up on the playing fields of necking and petting. But the big bugaboo of virginity was a settled matter

—as long as you kept it, intercourse and the whole style of life that is implied by it were out of the question. There were no myriad judgments to be made. Life was a juggling act, and so you juggled. If you know the younger generation, even if you have never read a survey or a poll, you know this is no longer true. Life is no longer crudely simple; it is subtly complicated.

The *Playboy* survey indicates that today the unmarried girl of twenty-five is more than twice as likely to have had intercourse as she was a generation ago. Kinsey reported that only one in ten of the young wives under twenty-five had engaged in extramarital coitus; today approximately 24 percent of that age group have sex outside of marriage. This is a meaningful shift. Virginity and fidelity are more and more becoming options and not ironclad mandates. Attitudes about virginity have changed quite radically in the group under thirty-five but still, 80 to 98 percent of husbands and wives seriously object to their partners having extramarital experiences. Enforced virginity as a prerequisite for marriage is now a matter of personal preference and not a command of society.

The contemporary youth approaching marriageable age does not see marriage as a gate through which he or she will inevitably pass on the way to an adult life and a career. More people get married today than ever before, a larger percentage that is, but marriage does not have its old inevitability. And it is by no means conceived to be the only way to have a full sex life. The positive dimension of this is that people get married because they want to get married and not because they want to have sex. Once married, as the attitudes of today's husbands and wives evidence, nobody accepts adultery. And an insignificant percentage of the married population engages in mate swapping, say 1 to 2 percent, and this may be limited to one experience.

It doesn't matter nearly as much today who's doing what with whom. What really matters is whether or not that relationship is honest, charitable, honorable, and responsible. In the light of contemporary values, if two men want to live together on these terms, a near majority of our population could regard their relationship as virtuous a relationship as any other. That is not to say that homosexuality appeals to this group or that they could justify it for themselves. It is interesting to note that no major surveys seem to indicate that homosexuality has increased since the mid-forties; it has just become more visible as the attitudes of society have changed.

Obviously, since age is the main factor in determining attitude and behavior, it is important to understand how teenagers are behaving, what they feel, and what sort of life-styles they are accepting. The key to where we are going in the foreseeable future lies in the realities of teenage life. Today's teenagers are exploring a new territory. We are witnessing the experiences of the first group since the Reformation who have been allowed to make independent and personal decisions about sex without fear of retribution. Consciousness has changed; perceptions are different; this is the frontier of the new American conscience.

Even if you are in a position to observe the life-styles of a great many teenagers, it is impossible to make assumptions about how all American teenagers are behaving. Fortunately, we have access to the results of a very comprehensive and highly scientific survey of Sexuality, Contraception, and Pregnancy among Young Unwed Females in the United States. The final report on never-married females, ages fifteen to nineteen, was written by Melvin Zelnik and John F. Kantner of Johns Hopkins University for the U.S. Commission on Population Growth and the American Future.[5] The field work for this report was done in 1971, and it involved 4,611 interviews with girls living in households and college dormitories in the continental United States.

This is an extraordinarily useful sample because it tells us exactly how unmarried girls were behaving in 1971 since every-

body interviewed was unmarried and between the ages of
fifteen and nineteen. In other words, they weren't women of all
ages recollecting behavior that took place over periods of varying permissiveness regarding sexual behavior. Strikingly, the
sexually *active* girls who had lost their virginity were not promiscuous; they were not even very active. Most of them had
had intercourse with only one partner, and not at all in the
month preceding the survey. In summary, Zelnik and Kantner
felt that these girls were poorly informed about the basic facts
of life and that those who never used contraception and those
who sometimes failed to use it constituted a solid majority. Even
among the sexually experienced, there was no indication of
rampant sexuality.

The pleasure-seeking female teenager with precocious mas-
tery of contraception is a familiar figure in contemporary media
coverage of the sexual revolution, but in reality she is a rarity.
The authors noted that half of all young women who had had
intercourse regarded it as a prelude to marriage, and if the
virgins were added to this group, those *saving* themselves for
the *right* man would constitute a majority. However, overall,
there was evidence of widespread sexuality. The sharpest increase in loss of virginity, a jump of over 50 percent, occurred
between the ages of fifteen and sixteen. The most significant
statistic was: 46.1 percent of girls nineteen years old had lost
their virginity.

The Johns Hopkins report offers data that supports the conclusions drawn from the *Playboy* survey. There is an increasing
amount of premarital intercourse, but most of it takes place
under the covenant of love and affection. As *Playboy* said,
"Premarital sex in a loving relationship still has marriage as its
implied goal."[6]

Sexual experience that is not accompanied by warmth and
affection troubles the conscience of the liberated young person.
Even college students who said that only about 3 percent of

their friends were virgins added that they did not respect women who slept with men of whom they were not fond. An attractive sorority girl in a Southern university said: "I don't know a person who will not sleep with anybody until they are married, but I don't know a handful of girls who sleep with boys they don't care for. It is a standard—a requirement of feeling." A graduate student in the Midwest said, "Everybody is doing it—it's not only accepted, it's almost mandatory. But," she added, "most of the girls I know would sleep only with boys they are fond of. And I know a lot of men like this—they just don't turn on unless they feel warmly about you."

A very bright and pretty girl in an Eastern women's college had thought a great deal about this question of a new morality. "It is a question of aesthetics, sensibility, and affection. Sexual intercourse is just not something you can handle as recreation. After all, it is truly creational." And any consideration that does not include a sense of the power and intimacy and real involvement of sexual union seems to misunderstand and underestimate sex itself. Obviously, a great many young people are introduced to sex before they are ready for it, and this has to do with personal development as well as the permissiveness of the times. The readiness of the individual and the fidelity of the situation are essential to any sort of satisfactory introduction to sex. Revolutions are successful only if they lead to a stable, tolerable way of life.

It is encouraging to know that sex itself has not been destroyed by this revolution. Not only have a great majority of the sexually active college students found that they have to be monogamous to maintain their emotional balance, but also an increasing number of young people experiment with sex and then back off. They discover that sexual intimacy is too powerful and complicated an experience for them to handle. In researching the sexual revolution in U.S. colleges and universities, Kenneth and Betty Woodward found that for many students sexual liberation has not been liberating at all. They write: "It now seems clear that after a period of promiscuous sexual experimentation, a growing number of young men and women are embracing what Columbia University psychiatrist Joel Moskowitz calls 'secondary virginity': a self-imposed chastity born of sexual disillusionment, insecurity and, oftentimes, emotional confusion."[7]

Accurate scientific polls and intelligent investigations, like the Woodwards', are immensely useful to us because they put us in contact with the reality of what is going on. Alfred Kinsey's monumental research actually discovered us sexually, located us for the first time. Until we get the truth, it is impossible to respond intelligently in this superheated and fateful area of life. Kinsey's work and the responsible research that has followed have militated against hypocrisy and deceit and uneven justice. Information doesn't encourage bad behavior; it supports the survival of the individual. It keeps perfectly normal people from thinking they are monsters or deviates. And for those of us who are deeply concerned for our children and our society, truth is kinder than speculation.

There is no simple truth about the sex lives of millions of people. But whatever happens from now on, I know that I have seen the end of an era. My personal journey has taken me from the cultic deprivations of Victorianism to a time of almost total individual freedom. Liberation day has come, and it is exactly the way getting out of prison has always been: a whiplash switch from stunting and obliterating oppression to bewildering and unmanageable personal responsibility. It's great to be outside here where everything goes, and you've got every right to destroy yourself. Making life accessible doesn't solve all problems; it just gives you the problem of living. As they say, living ain't easy and loving is twice as hard.

The old sense of sin is gone, or going fast. It is absolutely meaningless to the younger generation to tell them that they will be damned if they have sex before marriage. The old con-science that used to be bent double with guilt is psychologically unemployed and is being replaced, or recycled, anyway. Sin is still what it has always really been; it is being untrue or unfaith-ful to the best in ourselves and to the covenant that we have with other human beings.

The new American conscience is undertaking intricate, inti-mate considerations. It is coming together like music in re-hearsal; we cannot even imagine yet what its final effect will be. Somehow, it will process the ways that we respond to the splen-did and terrifying possibilities of this new life.

EPILOGUE

I have a lot of second thoughts about things, and this makes getting older a valuable process in its own right. Of course, I miss the past, but I've got it with me. Each of us is a limited edition of the chronicle of his time. More and more I can see the way elements of our experience are processed through our consciousnesses. As we grow older, we become more complete, more interesting in our content. If we can continue to get the truth out of life, we can stay close to reality. This will give us the vision to see how the clear morning of the future is going to break out of the turbulences of this afternoon.

Out of all of my experience comes an understanding of how life has affected me and how it has changed the way my mind works. What has happened to America for the last fifty years has happened to me. The great events of our national life have filtered through my consciousness in ways that are unique and in ways that are universal. I have stood on both sides of many great questions, and the forces of the half-century have buffeted me and turned my head around. How can I not believe in change when I am changed? I know that I am at a turning point in history because it has turned inside of my mind.

The account of my journey is the story of what's happened to me and what's happened to you and what's happened to America, which is all the same story. The closest we can ever come to understanding the mind of our age is to know what is happening inside of our own minds. From the beginning to this point we have passed through worlds that are gone. We are haunted by half-memories of missing faces and music and fulfillment. But the great purpose of this trip has little to do with the irrecoverable parts of the past. Our senses have gathered the essence of all of this, and it is part of our being; we are taking it with us up the climb, a great skein of evolving thought and imagery and sensorial imprint of all kinds.

In life, as in art, it is process that is important. In our innocence and in our wisdom, we process concepts and events over a long period of time through slow-gathered intelligence and understanding. Metaphorically, middle age is at the top of the ridge, has more view, and is further along in the process. The temptation of this age is to begin to think of dying, and the challenge is to begin to think of understanding life. As young people we are obsessed with the riddles of existence; when we are older, the passion quiets and the questions become clarified. It is not that enigmatic any more.

I have been through a continuous change of view of violence and greed and prejudice and hubris and lust. I see life very differently now, and having changed my mind, I know that I am going to change it again. In a sense we are all folks on a forced march, and we have to choose very carefully what sort of spiritual baggage we can load on this streak of energy. Some items are mutually exclusive. Obsessions are heavy. Things are heavy. Travel light. Take in the view. And carry the whole of your life experience along with you. This is a mystical journey, and the only true security is perceptual—it relies on staying close to reality which is changing all the time. As Albert Einstein said, "The most beautiful experience we can have is the mysterious."

We don't necessarily travel alone; I, for instance, have been helped along this journey by my traveling party. Three generations of us are strung out along the trail, and I hope to make it four before the end of the trip. My children, in their teens and twenties, have entirely different perceptions. They seemed almost to have been born to some of the insights that are fresh arrivals for me. Ahead of me is my mother, eighty, and she sees almost a century and has a folk memory that goes back much further. At one end of this spectrum, my mother conceives me to be a radical; at the other end my kids think I'm conservative.

Each generation sees life very differently and feels passionately about its own perspective. They are my blood, and I understand their feelings, and I am actually getting vibrations from the whole spectrum. Cumulatively we have eighty years in our grasp, and we are fairly evenly spaced. To me, we are a walking piece of history crossing the ridges and the knobs of the twentieth century. This is a wizard landscape. My mother can tell me where I've been, and the kids can tell me where I am going. If you look at us generationally, we represent sequential positions on many subjects. And I believe it is nature's design to inform man through this generational interlock.

With or without outriders, everybody is somewhere on this spectrum. We are all travelers. Each person is moving toward the present at a different rate of speed. And getting to the *present* is no small accomplishment. This is where the secret of prophecy is; prophets live in the present, and the rest of us are so far back that they seem to be talking about the future. I see that the motivation to move forward varies enormously. It is not entirely comfortable anywhere along the line. The consolation is that the most uncomfortable moments have new perspectives that bring an abundance of new awarenesses. I know that by an act of will I can grow and change as I get older, and coming to accept *the miracle of change* opens the consciousness just as the acceptance of any other miracle does.

You can see the whole progress of the metamorphosis of our sense of sin, of the evolution of our conscience, in this procession. The generations encompass a vast range of mindset from Victorian to tomorrow. Everything that has been working through the American conscience for the last hundred years is visible at various stages of maturation. To understand what is coming next, we have to see just exactly what is being processed now. There is every opportunity to do this if we can accept the information from reality, the truth.

If you can understand what is *true*, it is worth all of the pain that you could have endured during your journey. This is possible if you can use crisis and the battering of circumstance creatively to blast open new perceptions. Complex trauma is likely to produce the truth in slow-breaking revelations, and sometimes it comes out long, long after the fact. It is only through the mass and the momentum of the truth that we can break through to new solutions in *understanding* and in *works*. Once we understand the reality, we don't have to have a moral prescription to do the right thing. But it is as difficult to tell the truth as it is to accept it.

Occasionally comes a prophet who can hit you with the truth as though it were a bolt of lightning. Such a man was Dietrich Bonhoeffer, martyred by the Nazis at the end of World War II. "Telling the truth," Bonhoeffer said, "is not solely a matter of moral character: it is also a matter of correct appreciation of real situations and of serious reflections upon them . . . telling the truth is expressing the real in words."[1] And, of course, this is why the truth is so desperately feared.

Getting at the truth is a constant process of determining reality and then expressing what is real in words. Reality is constantly changing, being reconfigured almost minute to minute; so the truth isn't static, it is kinetic. The truthful word is not constant; it changes as swiftly as life itself. The great responsibility of the justice system is to find out what actually happened;

the obligation of the media is to portray reality, not to take a position on the tangled issues of this day. The conspiracy of evil is to hide and distort what is real. The fight against it in our society depends entirely on the relentless repetition of the truth.

The military example is the simplest: bombing civilians is "pacification of ambiant, nonmilitary personnel." When a combat photographer takes a picture of what is being described, that is, a naked little girl, half-cooked with napalm, running down a country road in Vietnam, you get the message from reality. Now, with that information in mind, you are in a position to make a decision either way about the bombing.

Obviously, the truth about Vietnam has been withheld by our government and then denied when reported by the press. And, yet, once the truth reached us, the people forced the United States out of that war. We could not stand the reality of what we were doing to that nation, to those people. This is the moral confrontation that we have with ourselves: if this is what it takes, forget it!

The whole experience of this war, building crisis of conscience on crisis of conscience, finally brought us crashing back to a reassessment of that enterprise that we call America. The result of this self-recognition is a rebirth of moral vision, a reclassification of good and evil.

There is this strange, historic echo. And then we remember that the principle of *truth,* of a free press, in America was central to the cluster of concepts that worked a miracle in the minds of the continentals. It created us and then helped us prevail. Our founders knew that the freedom of information could never be trusted to any leadership, and they said so. This instinct for our peril has been justified in our time.

If pride is the womb of all sins, then chauvinism is the name of pride. Finally, the human face emerges out of our great social and national conflicts, and it turns our minds around and changes our thinking. Whether the face is Vietnamese or black or woman, once we see it opposite us, we are confronted with staggering moral consequences. You can't push the button and drop the bombs; you can't condemn the human being to a soul-destroying disregard. You can't do this and save your own soul.

If we are buffeted enough, at some point we may see reality. This is the hope for us. There are striking examples of how positive understanding can come out of the ordeals that have seemed so destructive. This possibility is expressed by Egil Krogh, Jr., in his personal statement that was released after he was sentenced for his role in the Ellsberg break-in: "But however national security is defined," Krogh said, "I now see that none of the potential uses of the sought information could justify the invasion of the rights of the individuals that the break-in necessitated.

"The understanding I have come to is that these rights are the definition of our nation. To invade them unlawfully in the name of national security is to work a destructive force upon the nation, not to take protective measure."

Out of his own agony, Krogh has one admonition for young people going into government. "When contemplating a course of action," he says, "I hope they will never fail to ask, 'Is this right?' "[2]

Doomsayers have warned that if we seek the truth at any cost we will destroy our nation. Philosophers have charged that we have lost our sense of sin and can find no other. So, in effect, we are told that it is futile to make the necessary efforts to save our souls. This sort of rhetoric panders to the worst that is in us.

We are arrogant, self-righteous people, full of exaggerated pride, and salvation does not come easily for us. But, to an individual or to a nation, it comes the way you see it coming now. The doomsayers and the philosophers are wrong. Out of violence, out of hate, out of lust, out of greed, out of idolatry, out of chauvinism, out of all of this finally comes an imperative. **This is who you are. Accept it or change!**

Gunnar Myrdal, the great Swedish scholar and authority on American society, says, "American is the one country that can make radical change. I think it is the Puritan legacy. That has some bad inheritance in the way of self-righteousness and sex. . . . But, there is also the possibility of conversion: the sense that you are wrong and can change."[3]

Not only can change, *are changing*. America is into some painful self-knowledge, and we all feel it. Our minds have been jarred open, and we do have new perceptions. We are having all sorts of new awarenesses that will continue to surface, and we know that our sense of sin is moving along new pathways of conscience. On mighty issues, conscience has a late awakening. It must wait on alterations of perception. This is taking place.

Listen with your feelings and you can hear. All of the dissonance that rattles our composure is being formed into a new creation. What seems like wild disorder—the din of the blacks, the off-key brass of women's liberation, the jangled, discordant sounds of politics—is the harsh tuning-up of a new era. A new national spirit is being orchestrated. It is not audible yet, but we are coming into a new sort of harmony. We will not be in Eden, but we will be in a reborn society.

NOTES

1. VIOLENCE

1. The *New York Times*, Apr. 29, 1973.
2. Hopi Indian poster.

2. BUSINESS

1. Otto A. Bremer, "Is Business the Source of New Social Values?" *Harvard Business Review*, Nov.-Dec. 1971, p. 121.
2. Ibid., p. 122.
3. Quoted by James M. Gustafson, *The Church As Moral Decision Maker* (Philadelphia: United Church Press, 1970), p. 25.
4. The *New York Times*, Feb. 23, 1974.
5. R. Buckminster Fuller, *Playboy* interview, Feb. 1972, p. 195 ff.
6. Robert Townsend, chairman of the Executive Committee of Communications/Research/Machines, was formerly chairman of Avis Rent A Car. He is the author of *Up the Organization* (New York: Alfred A. Knopf, 1970).
7. Ibid., p. 201.
8. Quoted by Robert Townsend in his book review of *In the Name of Profit*, the *New York Times Book Review*, Apr. 30, 1972.
9. Quoted in the *New York Times* in response to the Energy Crisis.

3. POLITICS

1. Samuel Eliot Morison, *The Oxford History of the American People* (New York: Oxford University Press, 1965), p. 223.
2. Thomas Paine, *Common Sense* (Indianapolis-New York: Bobbs-Merrill, 1953), p. 19.
3. Ibid., p. 4.
4. Ibid., p. 32.

5. Ibid., p. 8.

6. Patrick Caddell in an interview with Anthony Lewis, the *New York Times,* Apr. 15, 1974.

7. Louis Harris, Harris Survey, the *Daily Times,* Mamaroneck, N.Y., Dec. 24, 1973.

8. "A White House Homily—Undelivered," editorial in *America,* July 21, 1973.

9. Ibid

6 SEX

1. Kenneth and Betty Woodward, "Why Young People Are Turning Away from Casual Sex," *McCall's,* Apr. 1974, p. 120.

2. Morton Hunt, "Sexual Behavior in the 1970's, *Playboy,* Oct. 1973, p. 88. (Researched by The Research Guild, Inc.).

3. Ibid., p. 200.

4. Ibid., p. 201.

5. Melvin Zelnik and John F. Kantner, "Sexuality, Contraception, and Pregnancy among Young Unwed Females in the United States" (Final Report on Population Growth and the American Future), 1972.

6. Morton Hunt, op. cit., p. 201.

7. Kenneth and Betty Woodward, op. cit., pp. 83, 118.

EPILOGUE

1. Dietrich Bonhoeffer, *Ethics* (New York: The Macmillan Company, 1965), p. 327.

2. Egil Krogh, the *New York Times,* Jan. 24, 1974.

3. Gunnar Myrdal in an interview with Anthony Lewis, the *New York Times,* June 24, 1972.